CANCEL THE APOCALYPSE

Thoughts from an Anarchist
Afrocentric Feminist
Nonviolent Revolutionary

ERIC S. PIOTROWSKI

Copyright © 2018 Eric S. Piotrowski

ISBN: 1-725-72494-4
ISBN-13: 978-17257-24945

Justified Textworks
just-text.org

Dedicated to

Pam
Milena
Inga
Yohan
Tom
Curt

Thank you for teaching me
the meaning of solidarity.

Hands up if you're confused — define tomorrow

Your belief system ain't louder than my car system

[…]

Each one teach one

The DJ spins a new philosophy into a barren mind

I can't front on it

*My head nods as if to clear the last image from an
    Etch-a-Sketch*

Something like Rakim said

Saul Williams
"Penny for a Thought" (2001)

CONTENTS

WHAT IT IS

This is a book about politics. Not parties and elections, but life, systems, and justice. It's a book about the stuff that moves me. The stuff that makes me burn with rage and glow with joy. This book is designed to provide insight and start conversation. I want to let people know where I'm coming from, and recruit folks to the struggle against injustice and oppression.

I don't have all the answers — or any answers, really. I'm just a guy trying to live a good life and fight back when things are messed up. I use lots of "I" statements in my writing because I try not to judge others, or tell people what to do. But I have ideas and perspectives that I want to share.

I want this book to afflict the comfortable, comfort the afflicted, fill in gaps, open minds, unbalance equations, and inspire hope.

I got so much trouble on my mind …

EVERYTHING IS POLITICAL

I am a political person, because every person is political — especially those of us who live in a democracy. Many people are worn out by the sad state of the world and the pathetic mediocrity that passes for political conversation in the United States.

Unfortunately, this leads many people to drop out of political life. They get uncomfortable when political disagreements surface; they think there's no way to have a mature, respectful conversation in such situations. Besides, there's probably nothing we can do about it all anyway, right? Let's just change the subject.

If you feel this way, I understand. But stick with me. I share your irritation with 21st-century political discourse, and I've had plenty of infuriating "discussions" that go nowhere. But I refuse to give up.

Here's why we shouldn't change the subject. First of all, it's simply not true that we can't change things. That's a matter of historical record, and I will prove it in the chapter on East Timor. As for being uncomfortable: While it's true that most political "conversation" in our society is shrill and bitter and partisan and pointless, we can do better. It *is* possible for humans to have sophisticated, respectful discussions about political issues. We can be passionate and emphatic, while keeping our minds open. We can dispute ideas without pointing fingers or calling names, right? Let's all agree to this right now. Deal?

Such discussions are, in fact, our duty as citizens in a democracy. If we the people are in charge of our government, then we have a responsibility to know about important issues, and demand that our elected officials take action. Part of political consciousness is talking about this stuff with the people around you — your friends, your co-workers, your neighbors.

The worst problem facing our democracy right now is the echo-chamber bubble in which most people hide away, hearing only those viewpoints they already agree with, and avoiding anything that challenges us. US Supreme Court Justice Antonin Scalia, for example, once told *New York* magazine that he didn't read the *Washington Post* because it's "so shrilly, shrilly liberal". Instead, he "skimmed" *The Wall Street Journal*, which is owned by Rupert Murdoch's News Corporation. He also listened to conservative talk radio, which is apparently less shrill.

This is a terrible way for any citizen in a democracy to act, and especially terrible for someone with the incredible honor and duty of sitting on our highest court. I read *The Wall Street Journal* all the time. I read it critically, and I get frustrated with its pro-business slant, but I won't hide from it. I can't take *Fox News* in large doses, but I visit their website once in a while. I work hard to escape my bubble.

There are two reasons for this. First, I want to make sure I'm responding to what these conservative sources are *actually* saying, rather than what I expect or remember hearing. There's a dangerous tendency for us to assume that we know what other people are saying — or would say — and therefore we think based on assumptions without going to the source.

But the other reason I read conservative sources is because I don't know everything, and my vision of the world isn't perfect. Every issue has multiple sides, and even my most trusted sources (like *Democracy Now!* and *The Intercept*) will occasionally leave things out of the conversation. Having an open mind means that you seek out different points of view, and take them seriously. As Chinua Achebe said in his 1987 novel *Anthills of the Savannah*: "Whatever you are is never enough; you must find a way to accept something, however small, from the other to make you whole and to save you from the mortal sin of righteousness and extremism."

The final reason I refuse to change the subject is because I can't. People are dying and suffering for no good reason, and I refuse to sit by while institutions of power cause such misery. Political prisoners are being tortured, and we can stop it. Women and men are being oppressed, and we can take action against it. Children live in poverty, suffering from hunger and despair, and we should end it. War and violence continue to ruin lives around the world, and we can do things to save lives. People call me naive and idealistic when I say these things, but I am neither. As Emma Goldman said in a 1912 lecture: "Every daring attempt to make a great change in existing conditions, every lofty vision of new possibilities for the human race, has been labelled utopian."

In fact, those cynical people who believe there's no chance for positive change are the ones who are deluded. Such change isn't easy, or quick, or automatic. It is not always fun. Working for change won't bring you love — although I met my wife through political activism. It won't bring you friends or wealth. (Those of us working for change are often working for change.) But change can and does happen, so long as we're willing to work and *make* it happen. As Frederick Douglass said in 1857: "If there is no struggle, there is no progress. Those who profess to favor freedom, and yet depreciate agitation, are men who want crops without plowing up the ground. They want rain without thunder and lightning. They want the ocean without the awful roar of its many waters."

Engaging in this kind of agitation doesn't guarantee that change will take place. But if you take no action, then you guarantee that change will *not* take place. It's easy to feel discouraged — I've felt the pain of political despair many times in my life. But we cannot let frustration prevent us from pushing forward. We should be skeptical, but not cynical. We should have not the optimism of Pollyanna, but instead embrace what Cornel West calls "a bloodstained hope".

In Lorraine Hansberry's 1959 play *A Raisin in the Sun*, the character Beneatha feels defeated and demoralized after her brother loses all of the family's money in a get-rich-quick scheme. She suggests to her Nigerian friend Joseph Asagai that all of human history is a circle:

> Don't you see there isn't any real progress, Asagai, there is only one large circle that we march in, around and around, each of us with

our own little picture in front of us — our own little mirage that we think is the future.

But Asagai knows better, and he makes clear that human history is in fact a line:

> It is simply a long line — as in geometry, you know — one that curves into infinity. And because we cannot see the end, we also cannot see how it — changes. And it is very odd, but those who see the changes — who dream, who will not give up — are called idealists ... and those who see only the circle — they call each other the "realists"!

You may call me an idealist if you wish, but I believe we are walking on a line which will lead us into a better tomorrow. It is not an easy path we walk, but we must not be discouraged by the setbacks and defeats.

Change happens slowly, and sometimes we move backward as a civilization. This causes some people to search for easy answers. "If only we did X," they say — abolish the police, end taxation, lower the voting age to five — "it would fix everything!" But that's not how things work. It's not sexy and it's not thrilling, but the truth is that the only way to fix the problems of our world is to work on it: educate each other, write letters, protest, call elected officials, boycott, get organized.

There's no easy way to lose weight, right? You just gotta eat less and exercise.

We must also understand that we can't change things by ourselves. We have to work with other people, in communities of consciousness and compassion. I have an instant rapport with people I meet who are engaged in serious political work. I know that we come from similar places, with a similar vision for the human family. One of the things I try to do in my fiction is reflect a world of political activism, where committed individuals work hard to make change happen. This is the world I live in, and it's a world that doesn't show up in movies or TV or comics very often. (Notable exceptions include *Persepolis* and *Promised Land*.)

Some people believe they're better off just staying out of politics altogether. Some people have been beaten down and disempowered. Other people don't know — or don't care — enough to get involved, so they just avoid all things political. I want to challenge this idea.

The truth is that our lives are political in every aspect, because politics have infused themselves into everything we do. The clothes you're wearing were manufactured in a process that was deeply political. They were probably made in a third-world sweatshop, just like the clothes I'm wearing. The computer on which I type these words — like your cellphone — was made using coltan, probably mined by exploited workers in a war zone. The fact that I have time to write this book is the result of political agitation, in the form of labor struggle which won me the right to leisure time, which was eventually enshrined in the Universal Declaration of Human Rights. (Article 24 — look it up!) The air we breathe is filled with particles (or kept clear of them) based on political decisions. Your job, my car, our food: All of these things have important political components. Life is not *only* a matter of politics, of course, but none of us can avoid them.

Besides, that's not a worthwhile goal to strive for. As Howard Zinn said in the title of his 1994 memoir: *You Can't Be Neutral on a Moving Train.* In other words, the status quo is pulling all of us in a particular direction, and refusing to take a side means you are, in effect, taking the side of the status quo. I refuse to accept the simplistic idea of "You're either with us or against us" — as Obi-Wan Kenobi says in *Star Wars Episode III*: "Only a Sith deals in absolutes." At the same time, however, we must recognize that silence benefits the powerful. Those Germans who quietly acquiesced to the rise of Nazi domination were wrong. Those white Americans who refused to protest the institution of slavery were wrong. Those Ottomans who silently accepted the extermination of Armenians, Assyrians, and Greeks were wrong.

Doing nothing is an abdication of our responsibility toward our fellow humans. Of course we have to protect ourselves, and different circumstances call for different responses. But it's too easy for us to ignore the suffering that goes on all the time, especially today with our personal environments flooded as they are with entertainment and spectacle. As Neil Postman said in the title of his 1985 book, many of us are *Amusing Ourselves to Death*.

Our ability to ignore the suffering of others is made possible by the death of empathy. We humans are naturally empathetic creatures. When a baby cries, our instinct is to make the crying stop. When we see someone in pain, we tend to ask what's wrong, and offer help. It's common, however, for people to lose this natural empathy over time. When a child is abused, for example, s/he often comes to view attachments as dangerous. When people are neglected, they may think that they have to care for themselves, and helping others will only get in their way.

The beauty of the human spirit is demonstrated in people who overcome those assaults on human dignity and commit themselves to preserving their connection to other humans. Powerful individuals like David Pelzer and Judi Bari and Debbie Morris prove that Shakespeare was right when he said mercy "droppeth as the gentle rain from heaven". (I'll discuss more examples of this phenomenon in a later section.)

Sometimes the sheer enormity of our world's ills can erode our empathy. *Another* homeless person? *More* political prisoners? A *new* war in the Middle East? It's easy to feel overwhelmed by it all, and it's tempting to shut down. But that's just another form of damage. We should take care of ourselves and step away from the news once in a while. But we should also stay engaged and let our natural connections to other humans flourish.

Finally, a word about Trump.

I wrote most of this book before the 2016 election, and I was involved in political activism for decades before Donald Trump became President of the United States. That election changed everything and nothing.

It changed everything, because some things in this country got worse. Hate crimes spiked sharply, and one of my good friends had to move to Canada, because her children weren't safe from anti-Muslim bullying. Our political divide has grown more hostile in the last two years, and some people have abandoned their connection to the world of facts.

The 2016 election changed nothing, however, because things weren't all that great before Trump was elected. War and poverty and racism and sexism and hatred toward LGBTQ folks was plenty awful in 2015.

Things look bad sometimes, I know. With climate change and nuclear weapons, it feels sometimes like we're in the countdown to armageddon. But despair is a luxury I cannot afford. Even if things look bleak, we never know what tomorrow may bring. (This is the same reason we can't get lazy and just hope everything will work out.)

Besides, I think we're gonna make it. Despite everything, I believe there are enough good people on all sides of the political spectrum for our civilization to walk back from the edge of catastrophe. I believe we can, as Saul Williams says, cancel the apocalypse.

We just have to keep working on it.

NO GANGS, NO DEBATE

Before I start wading into specific areas of political life, I want to urge everybody to think as individuals and members of a global human family, rather than the teams and gangs we usually align ourselves with.

Chris Rock said it well in his 2004 comedy album *Never Scared*:

> The whole country's got a f---ed up mentality. We all got a gang mentality [...] Everybody is so busy wanting to be down with a gang: "I'm a conservative!" "I'm a liberal!" "I'm a conservative!" It's bulls--t! Be a f---ing person. *Listen*. Let it swirl around your head. *Then* form your opinion.

This is more or less the same thing George Washington said in his 1796 farewell address:

> The alternate domination of one faction over another, sharpened by the spirit of revenge, natural to party dissension, which in different ages and countries has perpetrated the most horrid enormities, is itself a frightful despotism.

Being part of a political organization can be helpful, but it should not be our first or only allegiance. Our first allegiance should be to truth. We should never have just one group (or one person) to which we are loyal. We should be willing to dialogue with people from all over the world, regardless of their background or belief.

When I talk politics, I insist on what's called dialectical analysis. This concept goes back to the German philosopher Georg Wilhelm Friedrich Hegel, but it's basically the process of open dialogue. Dialectic conversations allow us to discuss things clearly as individuals, without clinging to orthodoxy or hive-mind groupthink.

I prefer dialectic to debate, because I want us all to learn and grow. The usual approach to debate pits two people with opposing ideas against one another in a winner-take-all form of rhetorical combat. Someone emerges as "the winner" and the other person is therefore a loser. This is the format of CNN's show *Crossfire*, and it's the approach most Americans take to political issues. It's one reason many people avoid discussing politics altogether.

Debate can be thrilling, and it's a valuable exercise in academic thinking. But I'm not interested in debate. I'm not here for academic thinking, I'm here to fight the power and find solutions. During a debate, the two sides bash heads until someone gives up or gets stomped. That's not how I want to spend my time.

Dialectic is different. Side A puts forth a point (thesis), and Side B responds with a counter-point (antithesis). Then both sides work to combine these points into a synthesis. That synthesis becomes the new thesis, someone creates a new antithesis, and the process continues. Ideally, each new successful synthesis allows us to elevate the discussion and find more common ground.

This is a more enlightened mode of dialogue, because it builds on the ideas and perspectives of everyone involved. At its best, it also removes the ego. If I say something erroneous, the other person isn't trying to pounce of my mistake — s/he merely seeks to point out the truth so that we can both elevate and operate from the same foundation of reality. Dialectical analysis therefore brings people together, rather than driving them apart, as traditional debate usually does. And whereas a traditional debate declares one side "the winner", in a dialectic conversation *everybody* wins.

The other benefit to dialectic is that it acknowledges (and encourages) the human capacity for change. It recognizes that our ideas and opinions and beliefs are not set in stone. (Grace Lee Boggs makes this point beautifully in the 2014 documentary film *American Revolutionary*.) Most of us believe what we're taught as children, but we always have the power — and the responsibility — to consider things from other points of view. When it's clear that we can't support our beliefs with good reasons, then we must reconsider them. We don't want to be wishy-washy or lacking in principle, but neither should we be rigid or closed-minded.

I'll use myself as an example. I used to support the death penalty. I believed that people who did horrible things like murder had given up their humanity and no longer deserved to live. I saw life imprisonment as insufficient, and the possibility of escape meant the threat would never be fully eliminated.

I don't know when I started to change my position, but I remember being powerfully affected by the 1995 movie *Dead Man Walking*, about the life and work of Sister Helen Prejean. Soon afterward, I saw her speak. I kept finding other important points made by opponents of the death penalty. I read an interview with Noam Chomsky in which he made a very simple point: "I don't think the state should have the power to kill people," he said. "I'm not willing to give the state that power." This made a lot of sense to me. Eventually I realized I could no longer support the death penalty.

Then I read the Universal Declaration of Human Rights, which says in Article Three: "Everyone has the right to life, liberty and security of person." This echoes the US Declaration of Independence, which claims the right of all people to "life, liberty, and the pursuit of happiness".

Along the way I learned many things about racial discrimination in death sentencing, wrongful convictions, and the power of mercy. I was further convinced by the 2004 documentary film *Deadline*, which follows Illinois Governor George Ryan as he decides whether or not to declare a moratorium on capital punishment in 2000. (Spoiler alert: He does.) I reviewed the work of The Innocence Project, a non-profit organization which has won the release of over 300 wrongfully-convicted people. Today I believe that the death penalty has no place in a civilized society.

Of course, my new position doesn't mean that I'm done thinking about it. People who have lost loved ones to violent crime often believe murderers deserve to die, and it's a tough point to refute. Dangerous people *can* escape from prison, and there's no easy answer to the question of what *should* be done with violent criminals.

It's possible that someone will present new evidence or a new way of thinking that will force me to reconsider in the future. But today I'm convinced that we should abolish the death penalty, as most industrialized nations have. According to a 2012 report from Amnesty International, only 57 of the world's 195 countries sentence people to death. In that year, the countries that executed the most prisoners were — in order — China, Iran, Iraq, Saudi Arabia, and the United States.

Although the death penalty is the issue I have most dramatically reconsidered, it's not the only one. And I'm not alone; many people are willing and able to re-examine their beliefs. It's healthy for us to question our assumptions and leave the door open to new ways of thinking. This is more likely to happen when we engage each other in open dialogue, rather than badgering people into agreement or silence.

Dialectic conversations are tough; they require special kinds of work. For one thing, we must assume that the other person is entering the discussion with good faith. (Many people who debate assume their opponents are lying or using tricks.) On the other hand, engaging in a dialectic *encourages* us to drop our facades and converse with other people in open and honest ways.

Having a dialogue can be especially tough when the other person wants to debate instead. In such situations, my favorite approach is simply to ask questions. Rather than pushing my own point of view explicitly, I will pose questions that seek to challenge the basis of the other perspective. My students *hate* this. They often respond, flustered, with: "You know what I mean!" Sometimes I do, but I still make them express the point clearly by themselves, rather than relying on guesswork and assumptions.

Here's a silly but useful example of a dialectic conversation in my classroom: I have a map of the world on the wall. After several weeks, someone will notice how I've hung it and ask: "Hey! Why's your map upside down?" I will ask: "How do you know it's upside down?"

"The words are upside down," the student will say. "Okay," I'll say. "Suppose there were no words. Would the map still be upside down?"

Students always insist that such a map would still be upside-down, and we discuss the tradition of placing north at the top of our maps, and what the concepts of "up" and "down" refer to anyway. Often I'll say something like: "Up is a conceptual fiction. There's no such thing as 'up'; there's only away from the Earth and toward the Earth."

Part of my intention is to use humor and make things difficult for the sake of discussion. But I'm *not* just "trolling", as the kids say. There *is* a point to be made here, one about epistemology and perspective. The way things have always been is not necessarily the way they *have* to be.

My map experiment is not really political, although maps serve many political purposes. My point is that our picture of the world *is* affected by our pictures of the world. Most of us have seen the famous "Blue Marble" photograph of our planet, taken in 1972 by the crew of the *Apollo 17* spacecraft. Chances are, however, that you've seen an *edited* version of that photo, with the planet rotated 180 degrees, to fit our usual view of the planet. In the original, Africa is "upside down".

Dialectic analysis lets us burrow through our assumptions and uncertainty, until we get to the essence of our different perspectives. It requires both sides to keep an open mind, but it rewards everybody involved with a higher level of thought.

So while the following discussions are filled with conviction and even bluster, please believe me when I say I am *not* promoting ideological assimilation or lockstep thinking. I want push-back and rebuttal, so long as it's done in good faith and with a spirit of building. I want other people to inject their own perspectives and opinions into these dialogues.

Okay, enough with the welcome mat. Let's get down to cases.

WHY I LOVE AMERICA

I love my country, but it is a conflicted love. The United States of America is a complex and diverse and confusing place, a place that is at times magnificent — and at times wretched.

The USA is my home, and I am eternally grateful for what it has given me. In the past I have forgotten the blessings this country has provided, and sometimes I have spoken too quickly and too narrowly about it.

Here I will speak slowly. I wish to explain how I feel, with words that are clear and careful. I want to consider the many emotions and memories and facts and realities and mythologies and conceptions and mortalities in my American mind. At times I must speak in generalizations, but I'll be careful. Please note that "America" actually refers to a pair of continents stretching from Alaska to Argentina. In the following discussion it is short for "The United States of America".

Let's begin with what I hate. I try not to use the word "hate" if I can avoid it. I worry that this word might upset some people, and I want to clarify (again) that I love the United States of America. But just as I hate certain tendencies and habits inside of myself, so too do I hate certain things about this nation.

I hate the violent racism of America. The trans-Atlantic slave trade, the theft of land and murder of native people. The internment of Japanese people, the anti-semitism within our borders. Hostility toward Latinx immigrants, stereotyping of other ethnic minorities.

I hate the male supremacy of our society. Rape, sexual assault, wife-beating, objectification, and feminized poverty. The hatred and exclusion of sexuality that doesn't fit into a narrow hetero-normative domain.

I hate imperialist US foreign policy. We supported the Indonesian occupation of East Timor for 25 years, which left more than 150,000 people dead. We supported the overthrow of Allende and Mossadegh, democratically-elected leaders, to be replaced by murderous tyrants. Smedley Butler's book *War is a Racket* should be required reading for anyone wishing to learn about US foreign policy. We invaded Iraq despite the lack of a clear and present danger, and caused between 100,000 and 1,000,000 Iraqis to die.

I hate the so-called "War on Drugs". We have allowed a repressive and violent caste system to take shape under the auspices of fighting crime. I hate the police brutality that so frequently accompanies law enforcement activity, especially in communities of color.

I hate the poverty and inequality all around us. In the richest nation in the history of the world, we allow children in six million households to go hungry. We treat medical care like a special privilege, rather than a basic human right. We allow desperate poverty to go on because we consider the poor less worthy. We don't care for our veterans, despite their noble service, when they return home. 37,800 veterans were homeless in January 2018, according to the Veterans Administration.

I hate American willful ignorance. 40% of us don't even know the Vice-President's name. Most Americans don't pay attention to events in countries like Afghanistan, where our sons and daughters are risking their lives every day. We have convinced ourselves that "American exceptionalism" means "We don't need to know about anyone else in the world". Sarah Palin was a serious candidate for the second-highest office in the land. Donald Trump was elected President in 2016.

I hate the tyrannical power of large corporations. In the last ten years Wall Street has committed massive fraud and criminal activity, and yet we've seen only a meager adjustment of regulation and virtually no legal action. There is a long history of capital hurting and killing workers in this country.

But of course the bad parts are never the whole story, and shame on those who pretend otherwise. As Friar Laurence says in *Romeo and Juliet*: "Within the infant rind of this small flower / Poison hath residence and medicine power ... / Two such opposed kings encamp them still / In man as well as herbs".

I could make a list of a million things that I love about America, and there's no question that a complete list here would easily overtake the previous list. (Thus my ability to say, in the final analysis, that I love America.) Still, here are a few items from the top.

I love the American spirit of resistance. Harriet Tubman, John Brown, Harvey Milk, bell hooks, Cornel West, Winona Laduke, Hugh Thompson, Cesar Chavez. These people — and millions of others like them, whose names we will never know — stood up to the evils of history and showed who we can be at our best.

I love American democracy and the Bill of Rights. Freedom of speech, protection from unwarranted search and seizure, free and fair elections. When I compare my political lot to that of most humans throughout history (and even at the present), I've got it pretty good.

I love the American spirit of individuality. Many other countries have a powerful emphasis on the collective will. I would not do well in such a society; my unique perspective on the world is dependent on an ability to express myself freely and protect myself from various harms. I love the American emphasis on the value of each individual's life, ideas, opinions, and security.

I love American art. Hip-hop is a uniquely American art form (with obvious roots in other cultures), and I love it with a deadly passion. Jazz soothes the soul and reflects so many beautiful things about our culture. Writers like Toni Morrison and Leslie Marmon Silko and Mark Leyner and Philip K Dick and Edwidge Danticat and Cormac McCarthy. Rock musicians like The Indigo Girls and Ministry and Consolidated.

I love the natural beauty of America. We have a breathtaking landscape in the US, including forests, lakes, mountains, prairies, beaches, parks, trails, and rivers. We're lucky to be surrounded by so much abundant nature.

I love the American sense of getting better. For all of our faults, I believe Americans want to heal. We want to get over the hatred and violence of the past. We want to come together and forgive each other and move forward into a better tomorrow.

For each of the above points, it's very easy to say "Yeah, but.." I must often force myself to stop the stream-of-consciousness "on the other hand" monologue constantly running through my head. Hopefully I have demonstrated my willingness to admit the sunshine *and* the darkness of our nation, in the spirit of confronting — honestly, but with love — all the various facets of this country.

Because true love doesn't blind itself to either truth. I don't want my wife to focus always and forever on what I'm doing well, what I'm good at, what makes her smile. I want her to be honest and let me know when I screw up, let me know when she disagrees with me, when I do something foolish or ignorant. We can't have one without the other — it just doesn't work for a long-term relationship.

And I'm in a long-term relationship with the United States of America. I can't sympathize with people who say "Oh, things are so bad. I'm going to move to Canada". (Although when President Trump was elected, the spike in hate crimes made a Muslim friend of mine take her family north. She felt the US was not safe for her children.) Those of us who love our country — and have the privilege to live freely — should stay here and fight to make it better.

Two of my best friends once gave me a superb comic book called *US: Uncle Sam*. It's a beautiful representation of my complex feelings toward America. I will end with a quote from that text.

> I won't deny that mistakes were made — even if the history textbooks do. But I won't pretend that mistakes never happened. And once in a while — sometimes very slowly — we made some progress. I tried my best to make people take pride in facing the problems. You're telling them to take pride in ignoring the problems.

Let's face our problems, my fellow Americans, and take pride in our ability to overcome them.

HOW I GOT TO BE LIKE THIS

My first taste of political consciousness came from rap music. I didn't know which power I was supposed to fight when Public Enemy chanted "Fight the Power" in 1989, but that song changed me forever. (I'm wearing a Public Enemy shirt as I write these words.) By devouring their lyrics and liner notes, I took PE's message to the next level and gained a better understanding of the people and events mentioned in the music.

Our parents raised my brother and me with liberal ideals of caring, compassion, and kindness. They taught for a living, spreading enlightenment and helping students who needed it. From them I learned about belief in action; practicing what you preach, and not preaching much. But when, in my teenage years, I found the world of political hip-hop — artists like Paris, KRS-ONE, Queen Latifah, Public Enemy, and Stetsasonic — I started to gain a profound new understanding of both the problems facing our civilization *and* the tradition of struggle working to solve them.

Another music group that deserves credit for my political maturation was a little-known industrial band from California called Consolidated. Combining noisy beats with pedantic diatribes against sexism, consumer culture, racism, homophobia, and a dozen other ills, their music hit me hard in a personal way. White rappers like 3rd Bass and The Beastie Boys had an attitude toward politics that was distant and tepid. Consolidated, on the other hand, went straight for the jugular in a fiery political assault. While I respected and admired African-American rappers, I knew that black life was something I did *not* understand first-hand, and I should never pretend to be something I wasn't. Consolidated showed me how white artists could challenge white supremacy, how men could challenge patriarchy, how straight folks could wage war on homophobia. If Public Enemy was Frederick Douglass, Consolidated became my William Lloyd Garrison.

The other early kindling in my political fireplace was a book by Ingrid Newkirk, executive director of People for the Ethical Treatment of Animals (PETA), called *Save the Animals: 101 Easy Things You Can Do.* (The cover art was drawn by Berkeley Breathed, creator of the comic strip *Bloom County,* one of my favorites.) I was shocked by its tales of animal abuse, deprivation, and suffering. More than this, however, the book simply asked me to consider my relationship to non-human animals, something I had never thought about before. What gives us the right to kill cows, in order to eat and wear them? Why is it okay to keep chickens in tiny cages? Why should makeup companies be allowed to experiment on rabbits and monkeys?

I became a vegetarian, beginning my commitment to animal rights. I knew it wouldn't make a big difference, but a couple of cows might be spared. I refuse to push my dietary politics on other people, and in recent years I have developed a deplorable weakness for seafood. But I still believe eating animals is wrong, and I encourage my students to question the food they've been fed all their lives. Meanwhile, it seems like PETA is doing everything in its power these days to make people hate them: shocking and guilt-tripping children, objectifying women to publicize cruelty to animals, and taking extreme positions that only discourage dialectic conversations.

More than anything, changing my diet was an immediate, concrete thing I could *do* to fight violence and oppression. All the other things I was learning about — police brutality, sexist violence, economic inequality, wars over resources and holy land — were far away and (I believed) impervious to the pathetic motions of a teenager in the suburbs. I shared my views with friends and published an oddball underground newsletter, but it felt like drops of nothing in the ocean.

In college I began reading Cornel West and bell hooks and Howard Zinn and (especially) Noam Chomsky. They provided a coherent picture of the world, with systematic analysis of history and current events. Unfortunately, I went too deep too fast, and everything came crashing down. I experienced a severe crisis of anxiety; for several days I was catatonic with existential pain and sadness. Everything was wrong, no one cared, and there was nothing I could do about it.

I was saved by the struggle to free East Timor. I will return to this story later on, but for now I will share two vital things from my work with the East Timor *Action* Network (ETAN): Concerned people around the world *can* make a difference; and those of us in the United States have a lot of power — and responsibility.

Along the way, I met a remarkable journalist named Allan Nairn. He had interviewed various officials in the Indonesian military, and had been told that if they received *one* letter from outside the country about a political prisoner, they would refrain from killing that person. I was blown away by the implications. One letter could literally save someone's life. This revelation encouraged me to get more involved with Amnesty International, writing letters to save lives and stop torture. I also founded an activist collective in college called WORD (Working On Real Designs), to help students looking to take action link up with groups looking for help. Our campus only had 600 students, and WORD was a tiny group, but we did some good work.

Also in college I met a superb professor named Paul Buchanan, who taught a class on revolutions. I was convinced by this time that small adjustments to existing conditions were not enough, and that more significant systematic change was necessary to end the suffering so common in the world. Professor Buchanan (who had participated in revolutionary movements in South America) said something one day in class that I will never forget. Rather than merely shuffling the arrangement of powerful people, he explained, the true purpose of a revolution is to uplift the consciousness of everyone involved. Otherwise, we just get a new batch of jerks at the top (usually using the same brutal tactics as the previous regime), and the deposed sector of society begins scheming to regain its power.

I am a revolutionary, because I've come to understand that adjusting the system (known as "reform-mongering") is not enough. Revolutionary thinking says that we humans can do better that what we've already established, in our structures of organization. This mode of analysis reaches into every sphere of political thought: We can (and should) create a better economic system. We can (and should) reformulate our conceptions of gender and sexuality. We can (and should) change our thinking about race in deep, systematic ways.

This revolutionary thinking must be enlightened, however — many of the institutions we humans have created are great and should be preserved. The US Constitution, flawed though it is, remains a solid document which we should honor and protect and improve. The United Nations is an excellent organization with lots of serious problems. Public schools in the US need to be dramatically improved in many ways, but the structure of free schooling for all people is a tremendous benefit for our society. An intelligent revolutionary makes distinctions between those areas of life which require systemic transformation and those which do not.

I will hasten to add the word nonviolent to this discussion, because many people associate revolutionary thinking with violent insurrection. I seek to place myself, instead, in the tradition of Mohandas Gandhi, Dorothy Day, and Martin Luther King Jr. Rather than perpetuate cycles of retribution and vengeance, I want to help everyone find new ways of being, in order to evolve our consciences and consciousness.

I see teaching as a radical political act. Not radical in the sense of storming the castle or overthrowing regimes, but radical in the sense of transforming mindsets and abolishing the ignorance that gives oppression its legitimacy. I don't force my political views on my students, of course. As Thich Nhat Hanh says in his *Fourteen Precepts of Engaged Buddhism*: "Do not force others, including children, by any means whatsoever, to adopt your views, whether by authority, threat, money, propaganda, or even education. However, through compassionate dialogue, help others renounce fanaticism and narrow-mindedness." In this manner, I insist that my students examine their assumptions and prejudices: Why is "feminist" a dirty word? What does affirmative action really mean, who benefits most, and what are the alternatives? How should a decent society be organized? What are the good and bad things about capitalism? As I tell the students all the time, they need to decide these things for themselves. They should not blindly accept what anyone tells them — myself included.

Instead, through simple Socratic questioning, I seek to jostle the worldviews of young people, just as mine was jostled. Although it can be unsettling at times, this process is necessary to bring about the insight and motivation to pursue truth and justice, freedom and peace.

In the third *Matrix* movie, The Oracle explains that The Architect cannot understand human decisions because he sees them as mere numbers in an equation. His purpose, she says, is to "balance the equation". When Neo asks what her purpose is, she says: "To unbalance it."

That is also my purpose.

I don't like the simplistic thinking that usually comes with political labels, but as Cornel West once said: "Categories are a compromise with chaos." Therefore I'm willing to identify myself as a feminist, an anti-capitalist anarchist (mostly), an Afrocentric multiculturalist, and a nonviolent warrior for justice and freedom. I am also a supporter of LGBTQ liberation, someone who insists on rights for disabled people, and (as noted) a vegetarian. I will address each of these issues in the pages ahead.

Two events marked the last big turn in my political life. Soon after I finished college, East Timor won its freedom and I started teaching. I have spent the last 15 years raising consciousness in the classroom and pursuing social justice in other contexts (sister-city solidarity work, assorted campaigns for human rights, and writing). There are times when my teaching isn't focused on making the world a better place; sometimes we have to study gerunds. But at the end of every year, I get some really nice letters from students, thanking me for helping them to see things in new ways and make sense of the world.

Finally, a word about privilege. I can tick every box on the privilege bingo card: I'm a well-to-do heterosexual cis-gendered white American guy living in a quiet residential neighborhood. I have plenty to eat, a loving wife, lots of video games, and time to enjoy them. The fact that I have the time (and the *chutzpah*) to write this book is itself an indication of my privilege.

There's a lot of talk about privilege these days. Some people think it's a way to silence discussion, or make others feel guilty. It's never been those things for me; instead, it's a way of recognizing what Donna Haraway calls "situated knowledge". Every person comes from a particular social and political context; some of us are born into contexts that bring certain benefits. If you win the lottery, you've got the privilege to quit your job. Being white gives me the privilege to easily survive encounters with the police. Being a guy gives me the privilege to speak my mind online without being sexually harassed. And so on.

This puts me into every "solidarity" camp, and very few "personal experience" camps. I'm a male feminist, a white anti-white-supremacist, an American internationalist, a materially comfortable opponent of capitalism, and an anarchist who orders around 125 teenagers every day. As you can imagine, this has led to some serious cognitive dissonance over the years. I must constantly balance where I'm from and where I want to go; long- and short-term thinking; and my own beliefs against the perspectives of others. I've had some awkward discussions about feminism with women who oppose every feminist principle I hold dear. Ditto poor people who love capitalism.

Still, we are one human family. The Chicago rapper Capital D once said: "My father taught me: 'Kid, be a man / Protect your family' / But what if my family / Is all of humanity?" Every division of race, gender, sexual preference, economic status, and social category is an artificial barrier between brothers and sisters and gender-nonbinary siblings. Thousands of hatreds and prejudices and -isms threaten to separate us, but one love can unite us and help us evolve as a species. If nothing else, this book is a quest to highlight the organizational methods of implementing that love.

The following chapters are in no particular order; there is no issue here that is more "central" or "fundamental" than another. We have to attack them all, together, at once.

WHY I'M A FEMINIST

Patriarchy sucks.

For thousands of years, human societies have structured themselves on a model of male dominance, with women ordered into tiny boxes of conformity and repression. But patriarchy forces men into cages too, so liberating women also helps men get free. Feminism has helped me come to a radical understanding of who I am as a guy, and I can't imagine being this comfortable in my own skin without it. Feminism is about challenging social gender norms, resisting domestic violence, giving women tools to take charge of their own lives.

Feminism is about equal rights, but with a conscious eye toward history and the nature of our dilemma. Feminism is about destroying patriarchy, because that's the source of gender oppression and inequality.

The best feminism is intersectional, looking at how gender, race, and other forms of oppression come together. Conscious feminists also fight against poverty and racism. Most feminists also work for the liberation of LGBTQ people. Most feminists challenge fanatical nationalism and repressive religious doctrine. Like many forms of political consciousness, feminism is more a process than a thing; it describes a way of approaching the world, with a focus on gender but no blind eyes to other systems of oppression.

Just to be clear: Oppression is different from other forms of suffering because it targets particular groups. Black people are oppressed in the United States *because* they are black in a white-supremacist society. Gay, lesbian, bisexual, and transgender people are oppressed in the United States *because* their sexuality and/or gender identity doesn't fit the norm. White people and heterosexual people and cisgendered people face problems too, but they are not oppressed in the same way as black folks and LGBTQ folks are.

Understanding patriarchy is the key to understanding feminism. Patriarchy is more than just men who beat their wives. It's more than just rape and objectification of women. It's more than unequal pay for equal work and sexual harassment on the job. Patriarchy is a system of thinking which allows all of these things to happen because it places male identity on a platform of supremacy. It is the system we've inherited after centuries of use, and as a result it's rooted deep within our collective psyche.

Thanks to the tireless work of feminists in the last 100 years, we've made great progress against patriarchal oppression. Domestic violence is no longer considered a taboo subject. Women have the right to vote, and the legal separations between men and women have mostly been dissolved in our society. Women have better access to health care than ever before, even while their reproductive rights are under constant assault. Our understanding of rape and sexual harassment has been improved, although sometimes it seems like we're not making much progress against those problems. The details vary dramatically in different parts of the world, of course, and it's hazardous to discuss all of human civilization in one breath.

Some people (mostly guys) think feminism has won all of its battles, and in some cases has gone too far. This school of thought says that men are now more oppressed than women, thanks to divorce law and social attitudes hostile to male identity. The more odious forms of this mindset have produced what is known as the "Men's Rights Movement", whose advocates call themselves MRAs. At the very least, they claim, feminism is misguided (or even dangerous) because it focuses on women's liberation, rather than simple equality between the sexes.

But this ignores history. Just as we cannot discuss race in our society without discussing centuries of violent white supremacy, we cannot discuss gender without discussing centuries of male domination. I wish male-female relations could be so easily remedied with a simple emphasis on equality. And of course, equality is the goal for which all feminists are striving. But I can't acquire a new car just by telling everyone that my 1998 Honda Civic is a 2018 Tesla Model S. I can't turn ramen noodles into lobster thermidor just by wishing it. In order to understand where we are, we need to look at where we've been, and deal honestly with reality.

Which is not to say men don't suffer in our society. I know men who have suffered the horrors of rape. Women can — and do — beat their husbands and boyfriends. Men are sometimes treated unfairly during divorce proceedings because of their Y chromosomes.

But patriarchal domination remains at the heart of gender inequality. As unfair as some legal processes might be, they do not outweigh the legacy of male supremacy or the attitude of male entitlement which permeates the culture. We can't erase centuries of patriarchy with 40 years of *Ms.* magazine.

Many people believe in feminist ideals — ending domestic violence, securing access to safe and legal abortion, guaranteeing equal pay for equal work — but won't apply The F Word to themselves. This is the unfortunate result of us feminists being demonized by popular culture. We're often portrayed as shrill, bitter people who hate men and wish to destroy the American family. But this is a horrible stereotype.

The feminists I know are warm, friendly people motivated by a deep love for humanity. Some of us get frustrated by the ignorance and violence that comes from patriarchal thinking, but why *should* we be patient in the face of that stuff? Of course some feminists become cynical and bitter, just as some Tea Party members are cynical and bitter. Every person from every walk of life has the potential to become cynical and bitter, and the ratio of cynical bitterness is no higher among feminists than among any other stripe of political identity.

So if you believe that patriarchy is wrong, and should be opposed in the name of freedom and equality for men and women, then guess what? You're a feminist. Welcome to the club. Come on in. There are many different kinds of feminism, and many ways to be a feminist.

My feminism manifests itself mostly in daily social interactions. I love to discuss feminist ideas online (although trolls make conversation difficult), and I enjoy challenging patriarchal assumptions in the classroom. Guys tend to talk more than women, for example. We tend to be louder, with deeper voices (that are more sonically powerful), and we tend to be more socially aggressive. So I encourage my male students to listen more, and I encourage my female students to talk more.

As a male person — one who suffers from severe logorrhea — this means I have to check my own tendency to babble, which isn't easy. Some young ladies will chatter constantly, of course, and I've had plenty of shy, quiet young men in my classes. As with everything, these matters are best handled on an individual basis, so long as we don't lose sight of the larger social patterns.

Although there are plenty of legal and institutional manifestations of patriarchy that must be abolished, I believe that the most important objective facing humanity right now is radically transforming what it means to be a man. We guys have to change our ideas about masculinity and gender in general, to fight against systems of privilege and oppression. John Stoltenberg took this idea to a new level with his 1989 book *Refusing to Be a Man*. I don't agree with everything he says, but he makes many important points.

The standard male psycho-sexual identity is flawed and stupid. It emphasizes domination and winning and forcing other people (especially women) into submission. It makes everything into a contest of strength and will, from work to marriage to friendship to parenthood. This sick identity distances us from the women in our lives, as well as from our fathers, our brothers, and our sons. We cling to myths of "alpha males" and live in constant fear of being weak.

Guys are scared to be vulnerable. We're afraid to give up control. We wait for our turn to speak — or interrupt — rather than actually listening to other people. We think that anyone who disagrees with us is stupid or ignorant, and there's no point in discussing anything so long as the other person doesn't "get it". Many guys overcompensate for their insecurities and turn to pompous projections of their supposed strength: Bulging muscles, powerful sportscars, enormous firearms, pretentious clothing.

Meanwhile, our culture thrives on the objectification of women — Hooters restaurant, *Maxim* magazine, advertising of all kinds, music videos, *Girls Gone Wild*. These images affect our thinking and contribute to negative body image among women and girls. They send the message that the primary value women have is through their bodies, so they better fit a specific type and be always accessible to men. Of course, as Jean Kilbourne points out in her excellent documentary *Killing Us Softly*, the feminine ideal is impossible to reach.

Besides, guys, this stuff makes us look like idiots. Can you be dragged around by your hormones and tricked into buying whatever some half-naked woman is holding or draped across? When a guy hires women to stand near him in bathing suits for a music video, doesn't that just make him look insecure? (And then we have the nerve to get mad at women who use their sexuality to get money!) Our fixation on impossible images of women as objects makes it look like we're incapable of honest interactions with actual women. And suppose you start a relationship with a "hot chick" because of how she looks — what will you do when her appearance inevitably changes? Will you toss her aside, using your wealth and status to acquire a new "hot chick", as many men do?

For those guys who avoid these horrible traps: Whether you think of yourself as a feminist or simply someone who believes in equality, you have a responsibility to help guide the next generation of boys into becoming men. For all of our talk about "family values" in the United States, we offer virtually no support for guys making this transition. We throw them in the deep end and hope they learn how to swim. Teenage guys absorb idiotic nonsense from movies and TV and the internet. Even supportive fathers usually don't discuss these matters directly.

Young men often see marriage and family as an inevitable fate that they have to delay for as long as possible. "Men never settle down," Chris Rock once joked, in one of his retrograde bits about gender. "We surrender." One idiotic t-shirt depicts a man and a woman at the altar with the caption: "Game Over".

Those middle years, then, are supposed to be packed with debauchery and conquest of women and flexing one's gendered superiority — and we think "boys will be boys". Of course there's nothing wrong with having fun. If you'd rather not get married, that's fine. The problem comes when "having fun" depends on the objectification and dehumanization of women, or dishonesty to avoid emotional responsibility.

This is an absurd, juvenile conception of manhood, and it leads many guys to mid-life crises when they decide they're missing out on some wild party existence they want to chase forever. But it's a trap of the patriarchy: If you accept a story about manhood that promises a constant parade of available women, you're bound to get stuck in a 12-year-old mindset filled with hostility and regret.

The worst manifestation of this pattern is the rise of the "incel" crowd, the supposedly "involuntary celibates". These men believe they are not receiving the intimacy they deserve, and they lash out at society, especially women — and *especially* feminists — for their sad, lonely lives. In chat rooms and online forums, they get together and reinforce their narrow mindsets of rage. It's the reprehensible but logical conclusion of patriarchal thinking based on power, dominance, and conquest.

Conscious adult men can help transform this process, by giving adolescent guys guidance and insight into living enlightened lives, without succumbing to asinine patterns of patriarchal thinking.

There are many other elements to sexism and misogyny. Women still do most of the housework and childcare, for example. Sexual violence is a plague on society, and more than 80% of victims are girls and women. Abortion and even contraception are getting harder to access, despite the fact that most Americans believe they should be available. We still haven't elected a woman president — although several women are running for the Democratic nomination as I write these words — and in 2019, women made up only 23.7% of the US Congress (25 of 100 Senators and 102 of 435 Representatives).

These things need to change. I'm committed to working, in small ways, to make that change happen. Being a feminist guy means listening more than I talk, and watching for those who want to speak. It means using my privilege to pass the mic to girls and women whose voices aren't being heard. It means challenging patriarchal nonsense when it appears in movies, video games, and comic books. It means never hiding behind anonymous screen names or social media platforms.

As the bumper sticker says, feminism is the radical notion that women are human beings.

ANARCHY IN THE USA

In a letter to his son Christopher in 1943, JRR Tolkien wrote:

> My political opinions lean more and more to Anarchy (philosophically understood, meaning abolition of control, not whiskered men with bombs) [...] The most improper job of any man [...] is bossing other men. Not one in a million is fit for it, and least of all those who seek the opportunity.

This crystallizes nicely why I am an anarchist. Put simply, I don't need people telling me what to do.

I've learned how to be a decent, intelligent, hardworking person who respects the rights of others and works to make the world a better place. I learned these things not through harsh punishment or bribery; I learned them from my loving parents, who nurtured me and set clear boundaries. I learned them from my awesome brother and my excellent friends, who helped me place myself in the world and understand who I am. I learned them from my indefatigable teachers, who taught me how to be a responsible individual, in addition to literary analysis and geometry and French conjugations.

In his song "Anarchy" (mixed by Ani DiFranco), the legendary folksinger Utah Phillips quoted his friend Ammon Hennacy, who once said: "An anarchist is anyone who doesn't need a cop to tell him what to do." Hennacy also described laws as useless at best: "The good people don't need 'em, and the bad people don't obey 'em, so what good are they?"

There are other definitions of anarchism, but basically it's the constant process of questioning authority. Is this authority legitimate? If so, it's good. If not, it should go away. Obviously a parent preventing a child from running into a busy street is using legitimate authority. An NYPD officer putting a pregnant woman in a chokehold because she asked questions about a barbecue is not using legitimate authority. (Yes, that really happened in 2014. Her name was Rosan Miller.)

I am *mostly* an anarchist, because I value some forms of authority among adults. A fundamentalist anarchist will demand the elimination of all authority everywhere, including police, military, and schools. I don't feel this way. There's no question that the police and military are fundamentally agents of state power, and they are used mostly to enforce a status quo that largely benefits wealthy elites. On the other hand, I do not believe — as many anarchists do — that police are mindless stormtroopers, doing only what The Man tells them to do. Through the demands of democratic citizenship, we have made police responsive in many ways to the needs of ordinary people.

Of course it's easy for me to think this way, because I've never had a negative interaction with the police. The constant surveillance, violence, and harassment experienced by O'Shea Jackson and TyRon Lewis and Rosan Miller are completely foreign to me. I understand why some people — especially black and brown folks — see the police as an occupying army, serving and protecting nobody in their neighborhoods.

As with all things, my anarchism is a matter of balance. All authority must, in every instance and every day, prove that it is legitimate. As Utah Phillips said, anarchy is more an adjective than a noun — it asks whether our institutions and interactions are going to rely on coercion or voluntary action. The most ill-fated and unacceptable interactions in human life are those based on force. Usually it's not gun-to-the-head violent force; we're often coerced into behaving in various ways because of economic forces, or social pressure, or the threat of punishment. Therefore we should structure our world — as much as possible — on voluntary associations, where every participant plays a meaningful role.

But anarchism is not just freedom; it's also focused on justice and equality. The boys in *Lord of the Flies* experience total freedom, but that's not the world anarchists aspire to. In that story, Jack turns away from his responsibilities to other people. This mindset of shared destiny is essential to the anarchist vision, and it is a mindset that is also *aided* by anarchist living. The more time we spend being coerced, the more we believe it's the only way for humans to interact. But the more voluntary interactions we enjoy, the more drawn we are to that form of interaction.

Of course, things are rarely so simple in reality. Once again, I will use my classroom as an example. For the most part, it is not a place of voluntary associations. The students are forced to be there. I make it very clear at the start of every class that I am in charge, and it is *not* a democracy. I have a tremendous responsibility to provide a quality education experience, and that doesn't usually happen if you let teenagers do whatever they want. A case could be made that schools would be better if we started all kids in a free environment, as proposed by Maria Montessori and John Dewey, then let them continue with free inquiry for the rest of their school days. But that's not the dynamic of the school where I teach, and suddenly offering such freedom is negligent at best.

As a new teacher, I tried to fully implement my anarchist ideals. I gave the students lots of freedom, and tried to nurture them in voluntary ways to follow a path of enlightenment. They did not. They saw me as a sucker who wouldn't care if they did nothing. So they did nothing. Worse, they goofed around loudly and got in the way of those who were trying to study and discuss literature. I met with unmotivated students individually, and tried to explain why English class is important. I tried to attack the root of their behavior. At the end of the day their behavior didn't change, and I left angry every day. Other students seethed with anger — more at my inability to create a good learning environment than the buffoonery of the unmotivated students.

So now I lay down the law on Day One. This is bizarre to me, because I hate being a disciplinarian. I hate using authority to control people. On the other hand, when I put my foot down and let them know that I won't tolerate nonsense, I have much better results. The discussions become more open and honest.

I know that my authority has limits; you cannot force a person to learn. Given the distractions and preoccupations that attack young people, I'm often amazed that I don't have *more* unmotivated students. At the same time, I've seen students move toward paths of education because of my encouragement and insistence.

Still, my approach is not one of blind authority. I haven't kicked a student out of the room in years. I talk loudly and sometimes pretend to get angry, but mostly I've learned to take a breath and recognize the limits of my power. The classroom is a strange place, where slacking off can be contagious. So letting a student do nothing is not wise.

I work with the kids in ways that are voluntary and not coercive. I would love to abolish grades — I studied as an undergraduate at New College of Florida, which has no grades. It was a perfect way for me to discover the true value of education. That's not how my school works, but I do what I can.

Aside from an introductory letter at the start of the semester, I don't bring parents into the discussion if I can help it. The students want to be treated like adults, and I'm happy to oblige them, so long as they handle their business.

Most people oppose specific forms of authority. Kids hate having adults tell them what to do. They especially hate the phrase "because I said so", and they're right to hate it. That phrase is a perfect example of illegitimate authority. A better alternative for the exhausted parent or teacher might be: "I can't explain right now, but please do it and we'll discuss the reasons later."

Workers hate having bosses tell them what to do. Many people hate having religious leaders tell them what to do. The Tea Party movement in the US has worked itself into paroxysms of rage about government authority, especially with regard to taxes and regulation. And so on.

Anarchism seeks to unify these attitudes into a holistic approach: Which forms of authority are legitimate? As Emma Goldman wrote in her 1917 book *Anarchism and Other Essays*:

> Anarchism, then, really stands for the liberation of the human mind from the dominion of religion; the liberation of the human body from the dominion of property; liberation from the shackles and restraint of government. Anarchism stands for a social order based on the free grouping of individuals for the purpose of producing real social

wealth; an order that will guarantee to every human being free access to the earth and full enjoyment of the necessities of life, according to individual desires, tastes, and inclinations.

I don't agree with Goldman on everything, especially her support for political violence, but she embodied many beautiful ideals that I share and celebrate. Her defense of anarchism is elegant and powerful.

As Tolkien noted, anarchism often gets a bad rep because violent individuals and angry, confused teenagers like to claim anarchy as their program. But there are many kinds of anarchists — just as there are many kinds of liberals, many kinds of conservatives, and many kinds of independents. This is a fault not of anarchism itself, but of the misguided purposes to which the banner is sometimes applied.

My anarchism is about compassion, enlightenment, and my intellectual obligations to other people. It's a philosophy of freedom and mutual uplift.

CAPITALISM IS IMMORAL

At its best, capitalism ignores human suffering. At its worst, capitalism requires and profits from human suffering. (To say nothing of the suffering of non-human animals.) Along the way, it relies on illegitimate authority from private economic power.

The basic premise behind capitalism is that private control of resources and freedom of markets are the best way for us to organize our society. At face value, that seems to match my anarchist convictions perfectly. However, freedom alone is not enough. When it comes to problems like war, starvation, suffering, pollution, and oppression, capitalism says: "Leave it to the market. The profit motive will find a way to address these problems." Only it never does, because there's more money to be made from junk food and land mines and erectile dysfunction pills.

Meanwhile, free markets lead to monopolies, corruption, slavery, and inequality. When there is no counter-balancing power to challenge the might of wealthy individuals and organizations — government, and/or labor unions — they run amok and cause chaos for the rest of us, as we saw in the crash of 2008.

Alan Greenspan has been a key US economic policy planner for decades. In some ways he was the poster boy for capitalism in the late 20th century. He was Chairman of the Federal Reserve for almost 20 years, starting in 1987, and his influence has been tremendous. Bob Woodward titled his 2001 book about Greenspan *The Maestro*. His approach has been one of free markets, privatization, and limited government regulation. In October 2008, when the size and significance of the crash were becoming clear, Greenspan testified before Congress. He confessed to a "flaw" in his ideology:

> I made a mistake in presuming that the self-interest of organizations, specifically banks and others, were such that they were best capable of protecting their own shareholders and their equity in the firms. [...]

> So the problem here is something which looked to be a very solid edifice, and, indeed a critical pillar to market competition and free markets, did break down. And I think that, as I said, shocked me. I still do not fully understand why it happened, and, obviously to the extent that I figure out where it happened

and why, I will change my views. [...] I found
a flaw in the model that I perceived as the
critical functioning structure that defines how
the world works.

Greenspan's comments strike at the heart of capitalism. Markets will not make things better if left to their own devices. They are not always the most efficient way of allocating resources or organizing human beings. In short, capitalism isn't good enough.

There's a reason the 1983 movie *Scarface* focuses on a young man coming to the US from communist Cuba; he seeks the capitalist dream of wealth and power, and he wins them with brutal violence. The same brutal violence was inflicted on workers at Ludlow, Colorado in 1914. The people of Bhopal, India experienced the same brutal violence in 1984. Many workers (especially in the global south) experience the slow-burning violence of poverty every day because of *lassez-faire* capitalism.

Wall Street's insatiable lust for profits is a root cause for many forms of misery. Executives at every company have a responsibility to produce profit for shareholders, period. Everything else is a diversion or a way to get more profits. So if workers are being paid poverty wages, but the company is making a good profit, there's no problem according to the standard capitalist model. Except there *is* a problem, for the workers. And since we're all part of one human family, there's a problem for the rest of us, too.

Besides, consider the dramatically unfair organization in your average corporation: The board of directors, usually 20 people or so, makes all of the major decisions. Imagine if 20 people made all of the decisions about our democracy. It might be more efficient, but it wouldn't be very democratic, would it? Alternatives to capitalism encourage us to imagine other ways of economic organization — worker cooperatives, community exchanges, and so on.

Many Americans recoil in horror when socialism is mentioned, but in fact we have enjoyed many benefits of socialism. Public schools are socialist institutions, as they should be. We use taxes to make sure that everyone gets to attend school. In some parts of the world, parents can't afford to pay school fees, so their kids can't go. The same is true about libraries and roads. Imagine having to pay ten cents every time you want to drive down Main Street!

The fire department is another example of socialism in action. For a long time firefighters were paid by insurance companies after a fire; if your house didn't have an insurance badge, the brigade wouldn't put out the fire. We realized, as a society, that this wasn't acceptable, and today everyone can count on the fire department in an emergency.

And then there's the internet. Despite the hard work from Jeff Bezos and Bill Gates, the internet is largely the result of socialism. For over 30 years, the Defense Advanced Research Projects Agency (part of the US Department of Defense) spent billions of our tax dollars to develop a decentralized system of computer network communication. As a result, we all now have email addresses and cute puppy GIFs.

Of course these things aren't perfect — schools in poor areas are often terrible. When Public Enemy recorded "911 is a Joke" in 1990, they called out the discrepancy between emergency response in white and black communities. Bureaucracy can make public institutions sluggish and horrible, as we've seen with recent scandals at Veterans Affairs hospitals.

But public institutions have a huge benefit over private ones: They are accountable to us. We can demand change from school boards and elected officials. The board of directors at a large corporation doesn't have to listen to us, unless we organize a class-action lawsuit or a boycott of millions. In a capitalist system, these private structures — tyrannies, essentially — do what they want to make the profits they need, and the rest of us have to deal with the aftershocks.

Please don't misunderstand me: There are some good things about capitalism. It gives us more choices as consumers. Of course, choice is only one part of economic life; I'd rather have two tasty choices on a menu than ten disgusting choices. Meanwhile, we consumers are often presented with health and safety risks under the guise of choice. When "caveat emptor" ("let the buyer beware") is the motto of an entire system, consumers who lack information — or money, or time — are going to get hurt.

Capitalism is sometimes tied to political freedom. Other times it's not. Some point to the collapse of the Venezuelan economy as the inevitable outcome of socialism. But Scandinavian countries like Denmark and Finland also offer socialist programs like universal health care and free college education. They're doing just fine.

Workers do often face repression in communist regimes, and giving a small government committee control over economic structures is problematic to say the least. This is why it's necessary to mix anarchism and into anti-capitalism. Replacing repressive corporate structures with repressive government structures is no way to make progress.

What we need is democracy throughout — ordinary people should be in charge of the government, the workers should be in charge of the workplace, and our institutions should be organized for freedom and justice, not profit for a few individuals.

As with every issue, it's important that we avoid orthodoxy and fundamentalism. In his 1967 book *Where Do We Go From Here?*, written one year before he was assassinated, Martin Luther King, Jr. addressed the question of economic systems with his usual eloquence and insight:

> Communism forgets that life is individual. Capitalism forgets that life is social, and the kingdom of brotherhood is found neither in the thesis of communism nor the antithesis of capitalism but in a higher synthesis. It is found in a higher synthesis that combines the truths of both.

I believe humans can do better than the current capitalist status quo. In a world as wealthy as ours, there's no reason for one person to go hungry. There's no reason for one working person to live in poverty. There's no reason for anyone to work more than 40 hours a week. There's no reason for people to spend decades repaying debt for education or medical bills.

It starts when we decide that our current systems aren't good enough. Then we can develop ways to make them better.

WHITE SUPREMACY KILLS

One thing that did change after the 2016 election of Donald Trump was a sharp increase in hate crimes. In many instances, those inflicting violence on people of color would invoke Trump's name while carrying out their hateful act. For more details, read the report "Ten Days After: Harassment and Intimidation in the Aftermath of the Election" from the Southern Poverty Law Center.

Like many Americans, I watched with anger and incredulity as neo-Nazis and white supremacists marched on Charlottesville, Virginia in August 2017. They carried out assaults against unarmed protestors — and some club-wielding anti-fascist groups — and murdered Heather Heyer. This was a terrifying example of the renewed force with which white supremacy was attacking our society. Fortunately, a follow-up "Unite the Right 2" rally in Washington DC one year later drew only two dozen weak-willed white supremacists, who were promptly laughed out of town by counter-protestors.

But white supremacy and racist violence are nothing new. In fact, the events in Charlottesville — and similar incidents in Berkeley and Huntington Beach — are just the most visible and disgusting public displays of a sickness as old as America itself.

Most people will agree right away that white supremacy is bad. Even "alt-right" white nationalist groups don't use the term. In fact, no one uses that phrase these days; most people prefer to use "racism" or "discrimination". These words feel less harsh, less accusatory. Unfortunately, they're also less precise.

Our modern conceptions of race didn't take shape around a vague attitude of some people being better at some things, or a few cultures having certain advantages. No, our modern conceptions of race were organized around a myth of white superiority and imposed with centuries of brutal violence, dehumanization, and oppression. This myth led to the Trans-Atlantic Slave Trade; the Nazi Holocaust; lynching and segregation in the US; and Apartheid in South Africa. It is a myth built on blood and lies.

It's tempting to think that the rise of certain black celebrities — athletes, movie stars, comedians, politicians, and business folk — suggest that we've finished this horrible part of our history, but things aren't so simple. The ascension of a few individuals doesn't erase the horrible legacy of white supremacy, especially when the material conditions of African-Americans — and black people around the world — right now remain unequal and unjust.

As with patriarchy, this history cannot be cleansed simply by wishing it away. It's lovely to see young white trying to live without prejudice, affirming their love for all people of all races. Seeing new generations rid themselves of the bitter hatred that plagued their grandparents is a wonderful thing. The abolition of legalized racial discrimination is a fantastic victory, won through intense struggle in the 20th century.

But it's not enough. Just because you treat everyone the same — and given the danger of unconscious bias, I'm always skeptical of people who make that claim — doesn't mean racism and white supremacy will just go away. We must confront institutional oppression and systematic discrimination. Once again, we can't be neutral on a moving train. The social, psychological, economic, and cultural effects of white supremacy still impact people today, and we must continue to fight them.

Michelle Alexander has laid out one example of white supremacy's continuing impact in her 2010 book

The New Jim Crow. It is one of the most important books ever written about race in America, and easily the most important in the 21st century. I would even say that you cannot understand race in America today without reading it. Alexander explains how the so-called "drug war" is in fact a new form of Jim Crow oppression, which imposes second-class citizenship on black communities. She points out that white and black people tend to use and sell drugs at the same rates, while law enforcement targets African-American communities disproportionately. This leads to harassment, intimidation, violence, imprisonment, and continual violations of human rights.

A "color-blind" mindset will ignore problems like this. Many well-intentioned white folks will proclaim their love for Martin Luther King Jr. and insist that a personal sense of equality is the best way for us to overcome the violence of historical racism. Meanwhile, African-Americans face disproportionate police brutality, decrepit schools, and unequal access to housing and employment. These atrocities must be actively resisted, and white people must be part of the fight. We have to recognize that, although we benefit from our white privilege, we are also hurt by these problems. Don't you want to live in a society where everyone is truly free and empowered? Systems of racialized violence are an affront to our human family and must therefore be abolished.

Some white folks bristle at the notion of "privilege", especially when they're struggling to make ends meet. Because of our predatory economic system, many working-class white people feel as though they're losing ground when communities of color do better. (This is a prominent mindset among Tea Party activists.) But this is a trick of the imagination, another manifestation of how we're all pitted against each other by the people who really run things. Those who control everything get those who have something to hate those who have nothing, so that we don't change anything.

White privilege is real, and we white people benefit from it. In 2003 researchers from the National Bureau of Economic Research sent out sets of identical resumes, some with names that sounded "white" and some that sounded "black". The results were dramatic, according to authors Marianne Bertrand and Sendhil Mullainathan: "White names receive 50 percent more callbacks for interviews." This is just one disturbing sign of white supremacy's lingering impact, and it demonstrates why a generic commitment to a "color-blind" mindset isn't enough. Those employers probably saw themselves as fair people who don't let race cloud their thinking. They probably weren't consciously choosing to hire only white people.

Affirmative action is one of the most controversial modern manifestations of race in the United States. Many white people consider it a *cause* of racial bias, rather than a response to it. But it's a necessary component of our democracy. Put simply, prejudice and institutional discrimination are realities in our world. Without affirmative action, black folks and other people of color will have less access to education and employment. Affirmative action isn't ideal, but it's better than the alternative.

Besides, people act as though college is a reward at the finish line of education, rather than another step on the journey of empowerment and opportunity. Why are there so few spots in colleges and universities to begin with? Shouldn't all people have access to an excellent university experience?

Race is a tough subject for discussion, because it can be flammable and toxic. As soon as the topic of race comes up, most people get tense. We worry that we're going to say the wrong thing and make somebody mad. For this reason, many white folks prefer to ignore or avoid discussions of race altogether.

But that's a classic example of white privilege. Black folks and Latinx folks and Asian folks don't have the luxury to forget about race, because our white-supremacist world reminds them of their difference every single day.

I learned early in life that I could not — would not — ignore or avoid the topic of race. The violence and suffering caused by white supremacy was too urgent. So I read Malcolm and Martin, marched against police brutality, and donated to organizations fighting the good fight.

Today I describe myself as Afrocentric for the simple reason that humanity itself comes from Africa, when we look at our global family tree. Africa has also been the target of white supremacy's worst atrocities, from military domination and genocide to the theft of slaves and severe economic exploitation. Like most Americans, I know almost nothing about Africa except what I see on the news about famine and war. Still, I try to broaden that vision by reading the work of African writers like Chinua Achebe and Chimamanda Ngozi Adichie; listening to African musicians like K'Naan and Doudou N'Diaye Rose; and consuming news from African journalists. If white supremacy was fixated on hating Africa with a unique passion, any attempt to resist and dismantle white supremacy should have a special focus on that continent and its diaspora.

Being a conscious white person has not been easy. I've had tense, angry arguments with good friends over issues of racial politics. I've often felt like an outcast from mainstream society, because I see racial oppression around every corner. And I never feel satisfied that I haven't done enough to resist white supremacy.

But guilt is not the same as consciousness. White people who feel bad about racism aren't effective activists. More to the point: If you're a white person who spends lots of time thinking about how guilty *you* feel, then you're continuing the pattern of focusing on yourself more than other people. I learned long ago that I needed to let go of those ego traps, and dedicate myself instead to the struggle against violence and oppression. The more real work I did, the less I worried about my white guilt.

Besides, we white folks need to recognize that whiteness itself has always been a trap. Before they were accepted as "white", Irish and Italian immigrants to the US were viewed with suspicion and hostility, much like immigrants from Mexico and South America today. Whiteness has long been a way to unify people based on absurdities, getting them to hate The Other and ignore the bonds of human connectivity.

Paradoxically, centuries of white supremacy in action have created a social reality that makes race impossible to ignore. As the motivational speaker Calvin Terrell says: "Race is science fiction, but social fact." I may not like thinking about things in terms of race, but I can't blame black folks like Mr. Terrell for making this point. I need to blame the architects of white supremacy who have poisoned our species.

Therefore race is a double-bind, because seeing things in terms of race is terrible, but it is also a reality that cannot be erased with wishful thinking. (Stephen Colbert has often ridiculed this mindset: "I don't see color," he once said. "People tell me I'm white, and I believe them, because I have my own TV show.") We *should* strive for a society in which race doesn't affect your life chances, but we cannot turn a blind eye to the ugly reality of today.

James Baldwin often critiqued the notion of whiteness in America, referring to it as an artificial construction designed to perpetuate dominance and privilege. In a 1984 piece in *Essence* magazine entitled "On Being White … And Other Lies", he wrote (referring to Americans of European ancestry): "Because

they think they are white, they cannot allow themselves
to be tormented by the suspicion that all men are
brothers."

It seems we must simultaneously acknowledge and
outgrow our whiteness. When I figure out how to do
both of these things at once, I'll let you know.

One of the trickiest problems related to race is the
inability to know what's going on in another person's
head. When police officer Jeronimo Yanez shot Philando
Castile to death in 2016, was he thinking horrible racist
things? Would he have treated a white person the same
way? We can never know. We can't say for sure that
because Castile was black — and Yanez is not — this
was a racist incident. But it's also wrong to assume that
race has nothing to do with the pattern of police
brutality inflicted constantly on black people.

James Baldwin also addressed this dilemma. In
1968 he said on The Dick Cavett Show:

> I don't know what most white people in this
> country feel. But I can only conclude what
> they feel from the state of their institutions. I
> don't know if white Christians hate Negroes
> or not, but I know we have a Christian church
> which is white and a Christian church which
> is black. I know, as Malcolm X once put it, the

most segregated hour in American life is high noon on Sunday. That says a great deal for me about a Christian nation. It means I can't afford to trust most white Christians, and I certainly cannot trust the Christian church.

I don't know whether the labor unions and their bosses really hate me — that doesn't matter — but I know I'm not in their union. I don't know whether the real estate lobby has anything against black people, but I know the real estate lobby is keeping me in the ghetto. I don't know if the board of education hates black people, but I know the textbooks they give my children to read and the schools we have to go to. Now, this is the evidence. You want me to make an act of faith, risking myself, my wife, my woman, my sister, my children on some idealism which you assure me exists in America, which I have never seen.

Anyone who is opposed to racism and white supremacy — really opposed — must wrestle honestly with the evidence and take action against the real conditions in the real world. We need to speak up and fight back, in all sorts of ways: by voting, by reading, by writing to elected officials, by spending (and investing) wisely.

Crucially, this is about reality and not appearances. Unfortunately, many white folks fret and fuss about how they look, and don't put in much actual work. If you spend more time worried about whether you appear racist than you do fighting against racism, your priorities are twisted.

Get it together.

WAR IS THE ENEMY

As the bumper sticker says: "War doesn't determine who's right, only who's left." Wars are dumb and 99% of them are based on lies. (The Gulf of Tonkin, WMDs in Iraq, et cetera.) Powerful men order soldiers to fight and die for noble reasons like patriotism and freedom, but inevitably it's just one group of young people murdering another group of young people who speak a different language. These people have no real beef with each other — they're just convinced that the other group wants to destroy them and their families and their way of life, so they have to kill and be killed by the millions. Meanwhile swarms of civilians get killed along the way.

Erich Maria Remarque's 1929 novel *Im Westen nichts Neues* (*All Quiet on the Western Front*) is perhaps the most important war novel of all time, along with Dalton Trumbo's 1939 classic *Johnny Got His Gun*. Remarque paints a horrid picture of his experiences in World War I; at one point his characters propose an alternative way of settling international disputes:

When asked by Jon Stewart to compare George Bush's escapades in Iraq with Christopher Columbus' voyage of exploitation and enslavement, Howard Zinn said with a grin: "Well, Columbus went *with* his men." As Michael Moore pointed out in his 2004 documentary film *Fahrenheit 9/11*, very few politicians who vote for war have family members in the military.

Most soldiers are coerced into killing and dying. In centuries past, a religious leader or a king would declare war for God and country, and soldiers would be tricked or pressured into killing other people, to defend some holy edict. Today religion still fans the flames of many conflicts, but economic pressure is also a key factor. We've done away with conscription in the US, but we have a kind of "back-door draft", where kids of non-wealthy parents often have no option after high school except to join the military. I once listened with a broken heart as a bright, motivated young woman explained to me that she had to join the military, rather than pursue a degree in international relations as she had intended, because she had no other way to pay for college.

We usually don't see the real horrors of war: The death, the mutilated men and women and children. The hunger and fear and suffering. Especially today, US journalists are embedded with soldiers and don't visit hospitals in Iraq or Afghanistan. But as Remarque wrote in *All Quiet*: "A hospital alone shows what war is." If you don't see the face of the child torn away by a bomb dropped from a drone strike, you can't know what it means for us to use drone warfare. After all, you cannot know the horror of Al Qaeda if you never saw the bodies of those killed on 9/11, right?

We don't pay much attention to the post-traumatic stress disorder that many vets experience when they return home. We like to watch wars end, and celebrate the troops' return, and move on. But as Tim O'Brien showed in his 1990 novel *The Things They Carried*, it doesn't work like that. (That book includes a story called "Sweetheart of the Song Tra Bong", which takes a fascinating look at war and masculinity.)

Wars fuel our hatred and fear. We think of people in Afghanistan as "the enemy", despite the fact that most of them are being oppressed and violated by the same jerks being hunted by US soldiers. War forces us to abandon our natural links to other people and forget about being part of one human family. Wars on foreign soil easily turn into occupations, and the positive reception our military may have enjoyed turns to animosity as the troops linger. (Even George W. Bush famously said, in a 2004 press conference about Iraq: "I wouldn't be happy if I were occupied either.")

Wars are usually revenge fantasies, masquerading as noble missions of justice. Let's be honest — Americans wanted revenge for 9/11, didn't we? Palestinians want revenge when Israeli snipers kill people, and Israelis want revenge when Palestinian suicide bombers kill people. Germans wanted revenge for the humiliating end of WWI, and right now Shia Muslims in Iraq are seeking revenge for decades of repression under Saddam Hussein's Ba'ath Party.

Wars have historically been fought for "freedom", and today we're told that war is necessary to stop terrorism. This is the reason Israel gives to justify its human rights abuses, and Bashar al-Assad says the same thing in Syria. But war can't stop terrorism any more than paintball can stop greed. Are we going to kill all the terrorists? It's a tremendously complicated subject, and those who commit acts of terrorism do so for many reasons. (To say nothing of how we *define* terrorism in the first place.) As Michael Franti says in a 2003 song: "You can bomb the world to pieces, but you can't bomb it into peace."

Malala Yousafzai was 15 years old when a Taliban gunman walked onto her schoolbus in Pakistan and shot her in the head, because she had spoken out for the rights of girls to be educated. She survived and continued her courageous work, opposing the use of warfare as a means to fight terrorism. As she said in a 2013 conversation with the World Bank: "The best way to fight terrorism is not through guns. It's through pens, books, teachers and schools."

War and terrorism are two sides of the same coin: Both have a misguided belief that more violence in the short term is the way to achieve less violence in the long term. But violence breeds violence. We can make the world a more peaceful place through international solidarity, helping ordinary people improve their lives, and rekindling the bond of shared destiny throughout our one human family.

Everyone says that violence and war should only be used as a "last resort". But people are usually ready to throw fists at the first sign of disrespect, road rage, or approaching stranger. Politicians brag about their love of diplomacy and peace, but their constant willingness to drop bombs and purchase bullets suggests otherwise.

Perhaps a military campaign is necessary once every century to stop a greater tragedy. World War II may be an example of this, although many important questions remain about the US firebombing of Dresden, to say nothing of our nuclear bombs. The problem comes when everybody insists the war they're supporting just *happens* to be that 1% exception to the rule.

Meanwhile, Americans celebrate war in a way that is unhealthy and dangerous. In our noble desire to honor those who serve the nation and put themselves in harms' way, we refrain from anything that might be seen as subtracting from that honor. This causes us to hide truths and turn away from ugly realities of US foreign policy.

For example: The 2003 US invasion of Iraq was an illegal and gruesome horror. Some of us tried to prevent it — and worked to stop the killing when it began. We were constantly accused of being unpatriotic, of hating the troops, of disrespecting the nation. Speaking only for myself, this was an especially unkind cut. It is precisely *because* I love the troops — including former students of mine — that I don't want to see them sent into a war based on misinformation. Of course, I love the people of Iraq too, because we're all part of one human family. I refuse to accept the idea that an Iraqi life is worth less than an American life.

Millions of us marched in the streets on 15 February 2003 to demand a stop to the US invasion plans. We were ignored. We marched and wrote letters and worked in other ways to end the war and occupation as it dragged on. We had small impacts along the way, but in 2019 there were still 5,200 US troops in Iraq.

Now that the war and occupation are over (sort of), we want to remind our fellow citizens of the incredible price — in money, in blood, in suffering — that were caused by this invasion. Over 4,000 US soldiers died, and over 100,000 Iraqi civilians were killed. These are conservative estimates, and don't count PTSD-related suicides, or amputations, of which there have been plenty. We want to help our neighbors and friends learn this history, so we don't repeat the same mistakes in the future. I am horrified when politicians today talk about invading Iran or North Korea.

General Smedley Butler was a decorated soldier in the US Marines. He fought in the Philippines, China, Central America, and France. He once got shot in the leg trying to save another soldier, and won a Medal of Honor for his actions in Mexico. After WWI, however, he decided that war was a deception that benefits powerful interests while massacring soldiers and civilians. In 1935 he gave a speech that was published under the title *War Is a Racket*:

> War is a racket. It always has been. It is possibly the oldest, easily the most profitable, surely the most vicious. It is the only one international in scope. It is the only one in which the profits are reckoned in dollars and the losses in lives.
>
> A racket is best described, I believe, as something that is not what it seems to the majority of the people. Only a small "inside" group knows what it is about. It is conducted for the benefit of the very few, at the expense of the very many. Out of war a few people make huge fortunes. [...] For a great many years, as a soldier, I had a suspicion that war was a racket; not until I retired to civil life did I fully realize it.

Butler's words presaged President Dwight Eisenhower's 1961 farewell address, which warned us of the "military-industrial complex" created by the "conjunction of an immense military establishment and a large arms industry", whose "total influence — economic, political, even spiritual — is felt in every city, every state house, every office of the federal government".

Unfortunately, our nation has not heeded Eisenhower's orders to "guard against the acquisition of unwarranted influence", and today weapons makers gain record profits while our young women and men in uniform suffer and die, alongside soldiers and civilians in foreign countries around the world. (For more details, please watch Eugene Jarecki's 2005 documentary film *Why We Fight*.)

The clergyman and activist AJ Muste spent his life fighting for an end to war and injustice. In a 1967 interview with the *New York Times*, he said: "There is no way to peace; peace is the way." And I'll end this chapter the same way I started it — with a bumper sticker: "You can no more win a war than you can win an earthquake."

EAST TIMOR: WHAT HAPPENED AND WHY IT MATTERS

Most people have never heard of East Timor, but it's an essential part of my life. I've been involved in East Timor solidarity for almost 20 years now. I met my wife through this work, and it has helped me understand the world and my place in it. I give a presentation about East Timor to my students every semester, and many of them insist it's their favorite activity.

Timor is a tiny island located 400 miles northwest of Australia, at the eastern end of the Indonesian archipelago. The western half of the island was a Dutch colony until 1945, when it became part of Indonesia. East Timor was a Portuguese colony for hundreds of years. Portugal exploited resources like coffee and sandalwood, but maintained a generally passive role. The colonial period led to an infusion of the Portuguese language, as well as conversion to Catholicism. Today, 90% of the population is Roman Catholic.

A 1974 coup in Portugal left East Timor with a power vacuum. The civil war that followed left several hundred people dead, and a left-leaning group called Fretilin declared an independent East Timor. Immediately, the Indonesian military — led by a dictator named Suharto who had come to power in 1965 by killing half a million people — began to prepare an invasion. During these early maneuvers, in October 1975, an Australian television reporter named Greg Shackleton and his four-man crew were reporting on the conflict in East Timor; they were killed by Indonesian troops.

On 6 December 1975, US President Gerald Ford and Secretary of State Henry Kissinger travelled to Jakarta, Indonesia, where they met with Suharto. During the meeting, Ford and Kissinger promised Indonesia that the US would not stand in the way of an invasion of East Timor. One person in the meeting said later that US officials "gave the green light" for the invasion. There was concern about the vast majority of Indonesia's weapons coming from the US, but the main worry was delaying the offensive until after Ford and Kissinger left.

The next day, 7 December, Indonesia invaded East Timor. Thousands of people were killed in the first weeks of the occupation, as the Indonesian military (TNI) began carrying out massive operations across the region. Rape was used as a method of torture and psychological terror. TNI soldiers spread out across the island, killing anyone suspected of belonging to Fretilin or other resistance organizations. 60,000 Timorese were killed in the first three months.

The United Nations did what it always does when one nation invades another: The General Assembly passed a resolution condemning the invasion and demanding that Indonesia withdraw immediately. However, the US ambassador to the UN at the time, Daniel Patrick Moynihan, worked to keep the UN from making this happen. In his 1980 memoir *A Dangerous Place*, he wrote:

> [T]he United States wished things to turn out as they did, and worked to bring this about. The Department of State desired that the United Nations prove utterly ineffective in whatever measures it undertook [with regard to the invasion of East Timor]. This task was given to me, and I carried it forward with not inconsiderable success.

In addition to blocking effective action at the UN, the United States provided 90% of the weapons used during the invasion. As the killings continued, TNI troops were trained by US forces, and US diplomats urged the world to ignore the bloodshed taking place in the name of anti-communism.

Indonesian generals expected to conquer East Timor in a single day. The expression used by soldiers was: "Breakfast in Dili [in the north], lunch in Baucau [in the central region], dinner in Lospalos [on the east coast]." The Indonesian military did not count on the incredible determination and will to freedom among the people of East Timor.

For the next 24 years, the Indonesian military carried out a brutal occupation, exhibiting all the worst possibilities of military oppression. Suspected resistance members were tortured constantly. Those who escaped the island told of massacres and bloodshed on an unthinkable scale. Disappearances and mutilations were common. A small-scale guerrilla force fought in the mountains, but resistance in the cities was forced underground.

The TNI carried out enforced starvation programs, denying food as a means to erode support for independence. Sterilization campaigns were carried out, injecting women with Depo-Provera. Migrants from various parts of Indonesia were encouraged to move to East Timor, in order to dilute the native population.

By the late 1980s, Amnesty International reported that 200,000 East Timorese men, women, and children had been killed — roughly a third of the pre-invasion population. News of the bloodshed was trickling out of East Timor, but the global community failed to take any concrete steps toward ending it.

In October of 1991, a East Timorese student named Sebastião Gomes was killed by Indonesian troops at the Motael Church in the capital city Dili. At this time, Portgual was preparing to send a parliamentary delegation to East Timor, in order to assess the situation there. The delegation was thwarted by the Indonesian military, but a number of foreign journalists — including Amy Goodman and Allan Nairn from the US — had traveled to East Timor to document the trip.

Sebastião's funeral took place on 12 November 1991. Seeing the presence of foreign journalists as a chance to get their message out to the world, members of the funeral procession began to wave flags and unfurl banners supporting independence. At the Santa Cruz Cemetery, the people held occupied Timor's first-ever public protest against the Indonesian occupation.

Unfortunately, the TNI responded as it so often did — with violence. Indonesian troops with M16s approached the unarmed protesters and opened fire. Over 200 people were killed in the cemetery that day, and another 200 were reportedly murdered in hospitals and other locations after being detained.

When Allan Nairn and Amy Goodman saw the soldiers approaching, they attempted to stand in the way, holding aloft their US passports as a warning. The soldiers attacked them, fracturing Nairn's skull and badly wounding Goodman. Meanwhile, British cameraman Max Stahl videotaped the massacre, hiding the tape inside a grave and smuggling it out later under the cover of night.

News of the massacre — especially the first-hand accounts from Nairn and Goodman, supplemented by Stahl's footage — shocked the world and revealed the hideous reality of life in occupied East Timor. The Timorese made it clear that such atrocities were *not* isolated incidents, as Indonesian officials claimed. The only difference this time was the presence of cameras. Within months, activists in the United States began to organize a group called The East Timor *Action* Network (ETAN).

Throughout the 90s, ETAN worked with the courageous people of East Timor to force Indonesia to end its bloody occupation. ETAN's primary goal was ending US support for this gruesome atrocity. Members lobbied Congress through mail and in person; a newsletter helped to share news and information; and new chapters sprang up all over the country. I organized a chapter in Florida, while my future wife — whom I did not meet until 1997 — was busy in Wisconsin doing similar work.

This activity was successful: Congress put an end to training programs, arms shipments were halted, and a proposed sale of F-16 planes to Indonesia was the focus of such criticism that Indonesia eventually withdrew its offer. ETAN continued to call for a referendum allowing East Timor to vote on its status, and pressured Congress to pass resolutions calling for the same.

In 1996, the Nobel Peace Prize was awarded to Bishop Carlos Ximenes Belo and José Ramos-Horta, two activists from East Timor, for their unwavering efforts toward a peaceful resolution to the bloodshed. This award renewed world attention to the plight of East Timor, and many activists in both Timor and the US felt a renewed sense of hope.

After General Suharto was forced out of office by massive protests in Indonesia, his successor BJ Habibie announced that the "pebble in our shoe" (as Foreign Minister Ali Alatas called it), East Timor, would be allowed to vote in a UN-sponsored referendum in August 1999. This was seen as a great victory for the people of East Timor.

Unfortunately, Indonesia also insisted on being in charge of security for the vote. While most international observers knew this was a bad idea, some politicians approved. They suggesting that the changing government of Indonesia should be allowed to prove its honorable intentions. But the TNI organized militia groups around East Timor, who began to terrorize the population. Militia leaders promised to destroy the country if independence was chosen; one boasted that "the streets will run red with blood".

In the shadow of these threats, the International Federation for East Timor (IFET) established an Observer Project, whose mission was to monitor and report on the conditions in East Timor, universally acknowledged to be far from free and/or fair. My wife was one such observer. I served in California as a US coordinator for the IFET Observer Project.

In April 1999, 200 people were killed at a church in Liquiça by an anti-independence militia group. Harassment, threats, and other acts of violence were reported all over the country.

Still, the people knew they would probably never get another chance to have their voice heard, so the vote took place on 30 August 1999. The response was overwhelming: 95% of the registered population went to the polls, and 78.5% voted for independence.

Immediately after the results were announced, the TNI made good on its threats; militia groups unleashed a new shockwave of violence through East Timor. International journalists fled, and the UN threatened to pull its staff out. A few courageous workers and journalists refused to leave the Dili compound, a site of refuge for hundreds of terrified Timorese. IFET was forced out as the killing began again.

At this time, the US refused to pressure Indonesia to call off its dogs of war. President Clinton's National Security Adviser, Sandy Berger, was asked by a reporter if we had an obligation to act on behalf of East Timor, given our recent action in Kosovo. He said in response: "[My daughter] has a very messy apartment up in college. Maybe I shouldn't intervene to have that cleaned up."

When the smoke cleared, thousands of East Timorese had been killed, and the country had been devastated. 70% of the buildings in Dili were burned to the ground. Once the TNI had destroyed everything it could reach, it approved a multinational peacekeeping force, and Indonesian soldiers finally left East Timor.

In 2002, after a short period of UN rule, East Timor declared its independence for a second time. The US solidarity community turned its attention to helping the Timorese rebuild their devastated country. Some people moved to Timor and helped to organize a group called *La'o Hamutuk* (*Walking Together*). Others — like our group in Wisconsin — created a sister-city alliance to promote mutual benefit and uplift.

Today East Timor is a very peaceful country, but also very poor. It is the poorest country in Asia, and one of the poorest in the world. Diseases like malaria ravage the population, and health care is almost nonexistent. Our group works with Dr. Dan Murphy, a native of Iowa who has been working tirelessly in East Timor for decades.

When I first got involved in East Timor solidarity work, some of my friends ridiculed my naive enthusiasm for the cause. "That's how the world works," they told me with cynical smiles. "You can't stop the US war machine." But they were wrong, and I told them so. Those of us who believed in peace and justice had a responsibility to take a stand. We did, and it worked. The people of East Timor won.

The story of East Timor is ultimately one of hope, but it's also one of nonviolent resistance. The leadership understood that they could not win an armed struggle against the Indonesian military, backed as it was by US weaponry and hardware. Meanwhile, the Timorese resistance received no aid from China or Russia, evaporating the myth of communist affiliation. More to the point, however, people in East Timor understood — like those in India — that nonviolent resistance offered a chance to transform their horrible situation, rather than merely shuffle the positions of power.

I was very lucky to be involved in the struggle to free East Timor. I have learned powerful things about courage, determination, and mercy from the Timorese people I have met. This work has given me an unshakable faith in the power of ordinary people to make change happen.

The victory in East Timor happened for many reasons, including simple good fortune. Many movements for freedom and peace are not successful. Tibet continues to suffer under the brutal rule of

Chinese violence, and Israel continues to occupy land seized illegally in 1967.

Still, the history of East Timor reminds us that change *can* happen when ordinary people care enough to make it happen. This story proves the lie of every slacker shrugging his shoulders and claiming we can't do anything about the world.

LOVE IS LOVE

No issue in the US has seen so much change so quickly as the struggle for the liberation of lesbian, gay, bisexual, transgender, queer, intersex, gender non-binary, asexual, and questioning people. (For the sake of simplicity I'll use the acronym LGBTQ.) In the last 20 years we have seen an end to the ban on homosexuals in the military, the legalization of gay marriage in all 50 states, and a shift in consciousness among non-LGBTQ Americans.

But we've still got a long way to go. As I write these words, the nation is reeling from a proposal from the Executive Branch of the federal government that would redefine the word "gender". This change would severely damage protections for transgender people that have been won through difficult and bitter struggle. Meanwhile, violence against LGBTQ folks is still a serious problem, especially for people of color. A 2017 report from the Center for the Study of Hate and Extremism found that hate crimes recently rose in major cities for four years in a row. LGBTQ individuals are often targeted for such attacks, and the center's director Brian Levin pointed out that among hate crimes committed against transgender people, "lots of these are extraordinarily violent". Bullying of LGBTQ teens is still a huge problem, and the CDC reports that LGBTQ youth are five times more likely than heterosexual and cisgender youth to attempt suicide.

These shocking statistics, important though they are, only tell us part of the story. The struggle for freedom and dignity among LGBTQ folks must overcome centuries of narrow, violent thinking about people who are different. Those of us who wish to be allies must confront our privilege and blind spots. We must continue to resist small-minded thinking and evolve our global consciousness on issues of gender and sexuality.

This isn't easy. For thousands of years, a particular view of gender and sexuality has been enforced with brutal dominance. LGBTQ folks have always been among us, but our society has forced them to lie and hide their true selves. Only after the 1969 Stonewall riots — which followed decades of organizing by the Society for Human Rights and the Mattachine Society — did America start wrestling with the violence caused by its narrow-mindedness. The Diagnostic and Statistical

Manual (DSM) of the American Psychological Association listed homosexuality as a mental disorder until 1973.

Ideas about gender and sexuality change slowly, because the roots of our thinking are deep. The most vocal and strident opponents of LGBTQ rights have usually come from religious circles, causing difficult conundrums for a nation supposedly dedicated to the separation of church and state.

But as 2007 film *For the Bible Tells Me So* explains, religious objection to the rights of LGBTQ people is an interpretation motivated by social and political ideology. Religious leaders — including Reverend Dr. Laurence C. Keene, Rabbi Brian Zachary Mayer, and Archbishop Desmond Tutu — appear in the film explaining the need for tolerance and understanding. The movie also tells the story of a mother who tried to force her daughter to hide and change her lesbian self. She experienced profound anguish and regret when her daughter committed suicide.

Objections to LGBTQ rights have nothing to do with what's "natural". The list of non-human animals displaying homosexual behavior includes the dolphin, panda, penguin, bluegill sunfish, desert tortoise, black-spotted frog, flour beetle, and box crab. And a 2016 article in *JSTOR Daily* points out that "many other species gain distinct advantages by projecting an appearance that doesn't 'match' their biological sex".

One important step is to recognize that our personal reactions to different people are usually based on emotional gut impulses. Those of us who wish to be allies in the struggle must be willing to honestly recognize these impulses, admit the injustice of policy based on them, and fight to end the violence they cause.

I've been guilty of these impulses myself. Once while visiting friends in San Francisco, I met a woman who had a goatee. Horrified of looking like a bigot, I said nothing and acted like I didn't notice. But inside I was freaking out. *Did I suddenly enter a circus?* I wondered. *Why is nobody commenting on this very unusual thing happening in front of us?*

It took me a few days to process this experience. I wish I could claim total woke superiority in the moment, but I can't. Besides, that desire is often a dangerous barrier for privileged folks confronting their own prejudices. So get over it.

Eventually I realized two very important things. First, that woman was very nice and interesting and friendly and cool. Her choice of facial hair — which was, let's be real, merely a decision to *not* ritualistically remove the hair that grows on the faces of many women — was not some harbinger of unsettling activity or a strange new world I had to live in.

Second, and more important: Her goatee had *nothing to do with me*. It was a choice of hers that did not affect me in any way, except to cause me a few moments of awkwardness. She wasn't hurting anybody and it was only the difference that made me uncomfortable. That was my problem, not hers.

Once I got over my own gut impulse, I was able to recognize my reaction as nonsensical. This allowed me to interrogate what had caused the impulse in the first place. I had never seen such a thing — except as part of a circus "freak show" — so I had no frame of reference for it as a normal, healthy choice. I started wondering why our society reacts with such hostility toward facial hair on women, which of course mirrors the hostility we have toward women's armpit hair and leg hair. We are trained from a very young age to think of these things as "gross", but that's every bit as arbitrary as thinking of men's chest hair as "manly".

So it is with all forms of gender expression and sexuality among consenting adults. We must each confront the squeamishness or hesitation we feel about people who are different. The ancient and illegitimate prejudices that cause these reactions are being smashed to bits, and we must continue — accelerate — the process.

It's tempting for Americans to get complacent about LGBTQ issues and rest on the laurels of recent progress. But the stigma endures, even if it's often cloaked in claims of "joking", internet trolling culture, or sarcasm. It's not enough to theoretically support the liberation of LGBTQ folks; we must live in ways that affirm the goal as essential to our own freedom and happiness.

We must be willing to challenge our assumptions and those of people around us. Here's an example from the world of politics: In 2008, Republican Presidential candidate John McCain responded to a white woman criticizing his opponent Barack Obama. "I can't trust Obama," the woman said. "He's an Arab."

McCain responded with an attempt to defend Obama in a way that was well-intentioned but problematic. "No ma'am," McCain said. "He's a decent family man, a citizen that I just happen to have disagreements with on fundamental issues."

As many commentators (especially Arabic folks) pointed out, McCain's response should have been: "So what if he *were* an Arab?" There's obviously no conflict between being an Arab and being a "decent family man", but McCain's privilege and background (involving, presumably, few interactions with Arabic people) led him to speak in a sketchy way.

We straight cis folks need to recognize that we do this on a regular basis. The prevalence of the phrase "no homo" among guys — fading though it might be — suggests that we are still uncomfortable with the mere suggestion that we have any hint of homo-erotic potential within us. The whole "real men wear pink" phenomenon still hints at a fixation on what it means to be a "real man", with specific color codes for easy identification. (I know, I know: It's shorthand for "real men aren't afraid to wear pink", which is a good thing. But it's still a way of encoding authentic masculinity based on clothing.) Real men reject artificial binary concepts of gender authenticity.

This occasionally shows up in my online life. I play a lot of *Rocket League,* a video game best described as soccer with rocket-powered cars. The online community is toxic: People (almost all of them male) ridicule and insult each other ruthlessly. Many epithets get users banned, but hateful guys online are very good at finding code words and loopholes.

Sometimes I play with a pink car with a rainbow flag that shoots out flowers. When a teammate scores, I will often type "YAAAS QUEEN" into the chat. This phrase isn't uniquely LGBTQ-centric, but it has strong ties to that community. I'm not trying to virtue-signal or be something I'm not; it's just one persona I use while having fun in the game. (I also have a car that spews frost; when a teammate scores, I write: "What an ice shot!") Over-the-top enthusiasm can be fun.

But not everybody sees it that way. Very often opponents — angry that we've scored, but channelling their frustration, presumably, into hatred of people who are different — will say "god ur gay".

I could respond with a quick and definitive insistence that I'm not. I could ignore their hate, and/or report it to the company. (I do the latter, although the company doesn't do enough to deal with these problems.) Usually, though, I try a limited, snarky form of consciousness-raising: "You say that like it's a bad thing," I write. I avoid the question itself, because it doesn't actually matter. Gender and sexuality are often performative anyway, so why do they care whether I actually prefer to snuggle with people of the same gender?

The point is that I'm not hurt by the "accusation". It shouldn't have the power to wound me, because being gay is not a bad thing. We all know this intellectually, but it can be tough to know it on a deep personal level. Until we all understand that truth deep down where it counts, our LGBTQ brothers and sisters and gender non-binary loved ones won't be free.

Straight and cis people have an especially important role to play in this struggle. LGBTQ folks have a hard enough time simply existing and loving themselves without adding the need to educate and enlighten the ignorant folks who wish them harm. We straight cis allies should never speak for those who can speak for themselves, but neither should we be afraid to speak up. We have to make clear that we cannot be free unless our LGBTQ loved ones are also free.

I've often wondered why it seems like we're making progress on LGBTQ issues more quickly than issues of misogyny or race. Maybe there's something unique about LGBTQ issues, or something uniquely powerful about the organizing strategies of LGBTQ activists that have yielded relatively speedy results.

Or maybe I only see quick progress because of my straight cis privilege. Maybe society is allowing superficial improvements that make it easier to continue deep forms of suffering and injustice. It's hard to say.

Either way, there's still a long road ahead of us to secure the freedom of LGBTQ people. I've had to walk some fine lines as an educator to make sure my LGBTQ students are safe — physically, psychically, emotionally, creatively, and socially — while not insulting or offending those who hold objections to their "lifestyle". I think (I hope) the lives of LGBTQ youth are less horrible now than they were 20 years ago. This doesn't allow me to let my guard down, of course, but I have books and movies to recommend that can provide forms of representation and ways of thinking that can be helpful. Such media can make a real difference.

Every one of us has a similar potential to impact the next generation. I can't tell you how many times I've heard a young person describe the power of an off-handed comment from a friend or family member. It's hard to overstate the power of language and the attitudes behind it.

My LGBTQ heroes — especially writers like Sarah Schulman, James Baldwin, Alison Bechdel, and Adrienne Rich — have provided us with liberatory languages and ways of thinking that have the power to set us all free. If you've never read their work, do yourself a favor and explore them soon. The themes in their work of love and freedom, accented by righteous anger, can help us all transform our thinking from gut impulses to conscious liberation.

HUMAN / NATURE

I became a vegetarian at the age of 14. At the local used bookstore I found a copy of *Save the Animals: 101 Easy Things You Can Do* by Ingrid Newkirk, founder of People for the Ethical Treatment of Animals (PETA). I devoured the book in three days, shocked by the wretched cruelty and wanton disrespect for suffering on display in every part of my life. I was alarmed by how little I had ever thought about such matters. I was forced to reconsider the food I ate, the clothes I wore, and the assumptions I carried. I dug into other essays, books, and documentary films. The deeper I dug, the more troubled I became.

I had been slowly emerging from a slumber of conscience for several years, aided primarily by hip-hop music. But this was a new frontier, and at the core of it lay one simple, disturbing question: What gives humans the right to kill other animals for their skin and flesh?

I decided there was no answer. As Peter Singer made clear in his 1975 book *Animal Liberation,* it cannot be our ability to do math or build bridges. We would never accept cannibalism of humans who cannot do these things, right? I had lived my whole life in a shroud of entitlement, where this question was never even asked. My parents were wonderful people; they simply raised me in a world of nutrition and diet based on the consensus of their time, aided by the best advice available to them from pediatric specialists.

Once I decided to stop eating meat, my folks were supportive but hesitant. My father explained that he had worked on a farm for many years, shoveling chicken poop. This, he said, had earned him the right to consume them all he wanted. This was not a glib dismissal of my position; it was more of an amusing way of saying "I'm not ready to confront all of that, and I don't think you are either." He passed away before I reached a level of maturity that would have enabled a more rigorous discussion.

My mother's main concern was for my health. She wanted to know where I would get protein and other necessary requirements. Addicted as I was to processed meals and junk foods with meat, I explained that there was no way cutting beef and chicken out of my diet could make me *less* healthy.

My decision to become a vegetarian was the first specific action I ever took to bring my politics to life. Of course I wanted to fight racism, but how many ways can a teenage kid in the suburbs do that? I wanted to smash patriarchy, but aside from complaining loudly to my friends about misogyny in rap videos, what could I do about it? Animal rights, on the other hand, was a cause I could take up right away — with gusto.

I knew at the start that my conscience *really* required me to become a vegan. If the widespread suffering and death required to raise meat were unacceptable to me, how could I abide similar cruelty to bring me eggs and milk? I had no answer, aside from: "They're so tasty, and I'm not ready for that level of commitment." Turns out, I never would be.

Part of this is due to the woeful inadequacy of substitutes. I have never missed hamburgers or chicken nuggets, because I live in a time where fake versions of these foods are plentiful and delicious. I don't think I could have been a vegetarian in the 1960s, when the only foods on offer were alfalfa sprouts and brown rice. Almond milk and vegan cheese are, alas, nasty. Tofu ice cream doesn't come close to the real thing.

I also decided, somewhere along the line, that I was too weak to avoid eating seafood. There's no philosophical distinction here; I'm just being hypocritical. Salmon and shrimp and clams are delicious, and — again — substitutes are disgusting. (I did have some tasty fake fish in a London pub in the summer of 2018, so we're making progress.) I try to avoid crabs and lobsters, for whatever that's worth. But I can't reconcile my love for seafood with my attempts to follow an ethical diet. So I accept the contradictions and try to do the best I can. Technically I should call myself a "pescatarian", but that word gives me a rash for aesthetic reasons.

I realized as a teenager, however, that the brand of in-your-face vegetarianism displayed by many PETA members was not for me. A friend of mine, whom we shall name Brian, was strident and insistent that everyone should follow his vegan path. He berated me for continuing to wear the leather belt I had owned for years. On a school trip, our bus stopped at a Burger King for lunch. Brian refused to eat anything at all, and scolded me for consuming french fries that were presumably cooked with beef fat.

The point, I decided, was that ethical purity was neither possible nor sensible. It was lunchtime; I was hungry. As for my belt: If I were the cow sacrificed to produce this clothing accessory, would I rather it be worn, or thrown into the trash? Neither option would bring me back to life, and I decided that — in addition to avoiding the purchase of leather belts whenever possible — the best way for me to honor this fallen cow would be to make use of its leather.

My father once told me that the Dalai Lama is a vegetarian, but will eat whatever food someone gives him while he is a guest in their home. This was a good reminder that our own personal ethical choices should never be the only consideration for how we act, especially when other people are making offerings of their time, resources, and kindness.

The other realization I came to, early in this process, was the systematic institutional scope of the problem. As individuals, we cannot will alternatives into existence. Fortunately, the last 20 years has seen a minor but significant shift in American society. Non-leather shoes are easier to find, and vegetarian foods are everywhere. This is surely due to market forces and not some profound transformation of consciousness. Still, it's a good sign.

My vegetarianism was driven also by an awareness that our planet's ecosystems are in crisis. John Robbins' 1987 book *Diet for a New America* showed me the links between meat production and environmental destruction, and I had one more good reason to make the switch. I knew that my turning away from Big Macs would not instantly save the planet, but it was another thing I could do here and now, along with recycling and riding my bike more.

In the 30 years since that book came out, however, the human emergency of environmental crisis has only grown more dire. I learned from George Carlin that I needed to avoid thinking of my mission as one to save the planet itself; it had endured plenty and could probably survive this latest phase of turmoil. The problem is that humans (and other lifeforms) cannot. It's more cumbersome to say "We need to save the habitat of our species" than to say "We need to save the Earth", but it's more accurate.

Unfortunately, accuracy and urgency haven't been enough to change the course of our civilization. Surely I don't need to recount here the dire effects of climate change we're already experiencing — flooding, fires, hurricanes, droughts, and other disasters. Climate change doesn't cause these, of course, but they are more frequent and more destructive as a result of humans pillaging the Earth's ecosystems. The problems are getting worse every year, while our political leaders bury their heads in the tar sands.

We need to transform our civilization's energy approach away from fossil fuels, and do it quickly. Some activists suggest that nuclear power is a sensible alternative, but the dangers of radioactive waste and potential meltdown make this an unsustainable choice. After the 1986 disaster at Chernobyl, supporters of nuclear power ridiculed anyone who used it as an example of why we should not build more nuclear plants in the US. That catastrophe happened, they said, because of Soviet ineptitude. It could never happen in an intelligent, technologically sophisticated capitalist nation like the US, Germany, or Japan. The 2011 disaster at Fukushima proved once and for all the silliness of that attitude.

Solar and wind power have their own problems, of course, and these technologies are not sufficiently powerful in 2018 to replace oil and gas completely in the US. Part of the reason is the incredible government subsidy poured into other forms of energy, while green tech has been ignored or hampered by government inaction.

But the fact remains that we Americans must make changes and use less energy. Why are so many of us still driving enormous SUVs when the violence to future generations is obvious? Why do we fill our homes with more and more energy-sucking gadgets? Roombas and

Alexas make our lives easier, but convenience cannot be our only consideration in this urgent time.

Obviously individual choice is a factor in making change — my wife and I have invested in solar panels on the roof and an electric car — but we can only do so much alone. And as tough as it may be for some fierce libertarians to accept, government restrictions on consumer freedom are necessary to save our species from total extinction.

Vegetarian living and recycling are good examples of small ways for individuals to make a tiny difference in the world, earning a warm feeling inside without transforming the horrible conditions that need immediate global attention. We've got to do more.

At the root of the ecological problem is a misunderstanding of the human's place in nature. We see ourselves as something different, something special. We consider it our divine right to plunder and exploit all of the planet's abundant resources, whether animal, vegetable, or mineral. This has brought some of us a wonderful standard of living filled with entertainment, luxury, convenience, and leisure. But these things are being financed with promissory notes against the air we breathe and the water we drink. Soon we shall have to make some painful choices to prevent a complete obliteration of our civilization.

The sooner we begin, the less painful it will be.

THE FALLACY OF EMPIRE'S INEPTITUDE

The activities of US imperialism have a very different character today than they did during our occupation of The Philippines, but it's hard to call our 2003 unilateral invasion of Iraq anything but imperialist. (If you're not familiar with the term "hegemony", now is a perfect time to do a bit of research into that concept.)

This new approach to expanding US influence, however — the so-called "velvet glove" around the "iron fist" — has been accompanied by two unusual approaches to international relations. The first is the appalling sense of amnesia experienced by powerful people when questioned by journalists or democratic forces. Ronald Reagan's use of "plausible denial" in the Iran-Contra Hearings was shocking but effective. He simply "could not recall" any relevant meetings, so he couldn't be blamed.

This phenomenon is related to the second development: The claim of ineptitude from incredibly powerful people and institutions. They insist that they are not responsible for horrible things done under their watch. Instead, it's a few "bad apples" that do their own thing, without informing the people at the top. Reagan claimed that Oliver North was acting entirely on his own, without any support from the White House. We saw the same thing in 2004, when a report on the abuses at Iraq's Abu Ghraib prison blamed a few US soldiers but not Secretary of Defense Donald Rumsfeld.

Which is worse: an evil and bloodthirsty government, which sees human rights as impediments, rather than sacred values; or a bumbling and boneheaded gang of idiots too stupid to take care of their business? I can't decide which is a more horrifying concept of our government.

Corporate America has adopted the same policy. We saw the exact same pattern in 2008, when one Wall Street executive after another told Congress that — despite their authoritarian control over thousands of workers — they had no idea that their Vice-Presidents were carrying out fraud and predatory activity in their firms.

Maybe we could enact a "Should Have Known" law. If you get to be in charge of a huge organization, and trusted with the responsibility of safeguarding the freedom and/or economic well-being of an entire nation, then maybe "I didn't know" isn't a good enough reaction. You should know about what your people are doing, shouldn't you? If my favorite student stabbed my least-favorite student, would people believe I were blameless, because I was facing the chalkboard? Note: I don't play favorites with students; and my classroom has whiteboards, not chalkboards. But you get the point.

I'm tired of hearing about how people in positions of power don't have to take responsibility for their actions, because they have underlings on whom they can pin the blame. Meanwhile, we hear constantly about how poor people need to have more "personal responsibility" and stop blaming others for their problems. Inept empires don't last. They collapse under the weight of their incompetence. The idea of any powerful empire being inept is a fallacious hoax, and I want everyone to stop accepting it as a legitimate response to accusations of wrongdoing.

Thank you.

WE NEED A REVOLUTION ON THE WAY TO THE REVOLUTION

Many political activists dream of a huge change that will fix "big" things, and they make other concerns seem irrelevant while we pursue the big change. "Once we achieve our great objective," this mindset says, "we can address the other, lesser, concerns." This paradigm is emblematic in the USA, to some degree — ours is a nation founded by white male slaveowners who claimed equal rights for all. But even in the struggle for abolition, for instance, male supremacy was everywhere. Racism reared its head in the women's suffrage movement. The struggle for LGBTQ rights has been plagued by lack of class consciousness. And so on.

Today, many of those waging war on tyranny, discrimination, and injustice continue to operate in the way of "our revolution first, all others second." Ralph Nader once busted a union at his publication

Multinational Monitor, and told the Washington Post in 1984:

> I don't think there is a role for unions in small nonprofit 'cause' organizations any more than … within a monastery or within a union [itself]. People shouldn't be in public-interest groups unless they believe in it and are ready to work for it. [Early in my career] I worked weekend after weekend after weekend…. Now people come here and say they want to fight polluters and unresponsive agencies, but not after 5 o'clock and not on weekends.

What type of noise is that? First of all, I daresay most of the people involved in such an organization probably do devote evenings and weekends to progressive causes — but they may want to diversify where their time goes. I teach during the day and often work for East Timor at night and on the weekends, for example.

But the real point is this: Our goal, if I may be so bold and succinct, is a world where no one *has* to work more than a fair and just 40-hour workweek. Right? So why can't we make that happen now? We can! We should.

When a small group (like Nader's) takes on an enormous institution (like a corporation or well-funded think tank), using more of the people power in the small group makes sense. But this must be done in a conscious and voluntary way.

The last thing I want to see is a fleet of burned-out, overworked, overwhelmed ex-revolutionaries who feel that the life of social change is just too exhausting. Besides, what vision of progressive life does this present to the next generation? "Sacrifice everything, or be a sellout." Some choice! This is exactly what Tupac Shakur saw when he considered what his mother gave up to join the struggle of the Black Panthers. It was a big part of why he rebelled against the activist path and got so lost in the club-party lifestyle.

Of course we have to sacrifice some things. You can't drive a Hummer and drink mimosas every day if you want to call yourself a revolutionary. But we are entitled to decent lives. We deserve time to relax and have fun! Article 24 in the Universal Declaration of Human Rights states: "Everyone has the right to rest and leisure, including reasonable limitation of working hours and periodic holidays with pay." Everyone, Ralph! Our world is wealthy enough — those of us fighting for truth, justice, and democracy are resourceful enough — to wage a conscious struggle in a conscious way.

There is always an algebra which must be calculated when the maximum effort must be spent to defeat the forces of darkness and suffering. But ultimately the level of sacrifice and dedication are personal decisions that must be made by each individual in a voluntary way. Brute, excessive force at an institutional level threatens to make us into the very darkness we despise.

This problem takes other forms, too. In the labor movements of US history, many women have complained that their struggle for equality has taken a back seat to what they're told is the "more important" fight for fair contracts. The media reform movement sometimes omits the perspectives and contributions of activists of color. And of course lesbian women and gay men still can't find the respect and inclusion they deserve, across the political spectrum.

Once again, the matter of raising consciousness must be central to all movements for a better world, not mere seizure of power. The point, therefore, is that we are all — every one of us — students in the class of consciousness. We must all be aware of our privileges and oppressions, and take conscious action to overcome them and/or keep them in check. More to the point, it means that while a more diffuse revolution may take longer and be infinitely more complex, it will also be more lasting, residual, and effective in the long run.

HOPE, MERCY, AND PROGRESS

The greatest enemy of humankind is not war or climate change or starvation — it's despair. Once people start to believe that there's no way for us to make things better, they stop working for change. Nothing makes powerful people happier than seeing the rest of us give up and go home.

The worst part of counterculture life in the 1960s and '70s was the popularity of the "take drugs and drop out" mindset. As if turning ourselves into zombies and nodding off were some sort of meaningful challenge to mainstream society. People use drugs to escape — whether it's alcohol or tetrahydrocannabinol or aspirin or TV or lysergic acid or social media or video games, we use these drugs to run away from abuse, or tedium, or pain, or something else. That's fine in small doses, but if you're taking pain meds every day, then you've got a drug problem. Nothing's going to change if you don't stop that guy from hitting you in the head with the hammer every morning.

So how do we keep fighting and resist the temptation to escape from our unpleasant reality? It has to start with hope. We have to understand that what we've got is not what we'll always have. We have to realize that right now is not all there will ever be. The past is not the future. We have to summon creative vision alongside an honest perception of current reality.

Some people in the movement live in a cloud of juvenile optimism. This is the facile mindset of the starry-eyed hippie: If we sing happy songs, then everything will get better. If we're all nice to people, then that kindness will spread and everything will get better. If I avoid being a jerk, then other people will be less jerky, and everything will get better. Unfortunately, this is only a minor step forward from a misguided attempt to be apolitical. While it's good to be kind to other people, it's not enough. While it's good to see the best in people, that vision will get shattered once the nasty realities of bloodshed, greed, and atrocity start to seep under the door. (And they will.)

The river is a useful metaphor here. Utah Phillips once explained the importance of resistance: "If you don't learn to resist," he said, "you take the path of least resistance. And taking the path of least resistance is what makes the river crooked." Sometimes, though, we're affected by the river, rather than being it. In the Coen Brothers' 1991 classic film *Barton Fink*, the character WP Mayhew explains why he drinks: "I'm buildin' a levee. Puttin' up a levee to keep that ragin' river of manure from lappin' at my door." It's easy to feel like the "raging river of manure" that is the world's suffering and pain will soon overwhelm us. We all need levees to keep the horrors away, if only for a little while. But the strongest levees are made of stress management and consciousness, not alcohol or other drugs.

Another source of hope is the amazing grace shown by people who have forgiven those who have hurt them or their loved ones. We're all familiar with the power of forgiveness shown by people like Martin Luther King and Mohandas Gandhi (not to mention Jesus of Nazareth). I want to call your attention to some other examples of breathtaking mercy.

Debbie Morris was abducted with her boyfriend Mark by two men. They killed Mark and raped her numerous times. She escaped and hoped to find closure when one of her attackers was executed by the state of Louisiana. (His relationship with Sister Helen Prejean was the subject of the 1996 movie *Dead Man Walking*.) Eventually, however, Morris realized that she was not reaching peace through her anger, and decided to forgive the man. She wrote about her experiences in the 2000 book *Forgiving the Dead Man Walking*.

Phyllis Rodriguez lost her son Greg in the terrorist attacks of 9/11. She was devastated, but felt pangs of sympathy when she saw **Aicha el-Wafi**, the mother of 9/11 conspirator Zacarias Moussaoui, suffering her own grief. She reached out to Aicha and they became friends. Rodriguez opposed the death penalty for Moussaoui, saying: "When I watched Zacarias at the trial my heart was broken because I could not look at him as a stranger. I saw him as the son of my friend Aicha." The story of Phyllis Rodriguez and her husband Orlando is told in the 2016 documentary film *In Our Son's Name*.

Rais Bhuiyan was working at a convenience store in October 2001 when Mark Anthony Stroman shot him in the face with a shotgun as part of a killing spree in revenge for 9/11. Bhuiyan forgave Stroman — who later renounced his white supremacist views — and spoke out against his attacker's death penalty sentence. "I forgive you," Bhuiyan told Stroman just before the execution, "and I do not hate you." In 2017 Bhuiyan told his story in a talk at TEDxEmory called *The Magic of Humanity: Forgiveness, Mercy, and Compassion*.

Eva Mozes Kor was taken to Auschwitz at the age of 10 and subjected — with her twin sister — to atrocious medical experiments at the hands of Josef Mengele. She survived and eventually forgave the Nazis for what they did to her and her family. In 1995 she founded the CANDLES [Children of Auschwitz Nazi Deadly Lab Experiments Survivors] Museum in Indiana. In the 2006 documentary film *Forgiving Dr. Mengele*, she said: "Forgive your worst enemy. It will heal your soul, and it will set you free."

The Amish community in **Nickel Mines, Pennsylvania** was devastated in 2006 when a gunman entered a schoolhouse, shot ten girls — killing five — and committed suicide. The grandfather of one of the murdered girls warned his family not to let hatred cloud their thinking: "We must not think evil of this man," he said. The community offered forgiveness to the man, comforted his parents, and set up a charitable fund for his widow and children. Parents of two of the murdered girls attended the man's funeral and offered words of comfort to his mother. In 2013, she told CBS News: "Wow. Is there anything in this life we should not forgive?" The story of Nickel Mines is told in the 2007 book *Amish Grace: How Forgiveness Transcended Tragedy*.

Abdollah Hosseinzadeh was stabbed to death in a 2007 street fight in Royan, Iran. In April 2014 his mother was scheduled to participate in the public execution of his killer. Instead, she slapped the young man in the face, declared her forgiveness, and ordered Abdollah's father to remove the noose. Then she hugged the mother of her son's killer, both of them crying.

Forgiveness does not mean forgetting. It is an act of healing, focused as much on relieving our own pain as the suffering of others. Mercy 7does not obliterate the horrible things done by other people, or pretend they never happened. It seeks to cure the root of the pain, through love and compassion rather than retribution or revenge.

If these amazing people can endure such horrible violence and still find the grace to forgive those responsible, how can the rest of us let hatred and despair cloud our minds? How can I stay mad at the jerk who cut me off in traffic? How can we believe that things can't get better, when these brave women and men show us the transcendent power of mercy?

The plain fact of human existence is that we can heal, both as individuals and as a species. The only question is what part each of us will play in this process, and how long it will take.

GOOD POLITICAL MOVIES

Because Hollywood is a left-leaning community, it has produced some good work dealing with issues of sociology and politics. In fact, given their popularity, movies have the power to influence attitudes like no other media. *The Accused* changed our national discourse about rape. *The China Syndrome* shed important light on the dangers of nuclear power. *Network* broke important ground on journalism and the power of TV. Everyone knows the famous speech from that movie about "I want you to go to your window and open it and yell 'I'm mad as hell, and I'm not going to take it anymore!'". But later in the movie there's an even better speech about how "There is no America".

Most Hollywood movies are mild in their politics, and in the 21st century producers have realized that political themes can alienate large parts of their audience. Most of the time this means that political elements are very generic, as we saw in *Avatar*. Which was simply a retelling of Disney's *Pocahontas*, which was itself a retelling of *Dances With Wolves*, etc etc. I'm amused to see Disney lecturing us with lyrics like

"Come roll in all the riches all around you / And for once, never wonder what they're worth" while that company slaps copyright on every public-domain story ever made, and produces endless rivers of cheap consumer crap in third-world sweatshops.

My other big gripe with Hollywood's political movies is that they always put a straight white guy in the center of the story, even when the story is about war in Africa (*Blood Diamond*), or slavery in the US (*Amistad*), or the early days of the AIDS crisis (*Dallas Buyers Club*). These aren't bad movies, and sometimes they make valuable contributions to the discussion of their issues. But the idea that audiences won't relate to a story unless it features a straight white dude assumes that (a) straight white people are never interested in anyone other than themselves, and (b) the audience consists of nothing but straight white guys. Both of these ideas are idiotic.

I could go on forever complaining about Hollywood's shortcomings — if you're not familiar with The Bechdel Test, check out the *Feminist Frequency* video about it — but I want to offer my kudos to quality films dealing with political issues. Here they are, in no particular order:

The Corporation (2003) is the best documentary film ever made. It's really entertaining, and it's got interviews with people from all walks of life (CEOs, working shmoes, average janes and joes). It has a simple question at its heart: If corporations are people, then what kind of people are they? It uses the World Health Organization's checklist for psychopathology to demonstrate just how dysfunctional the modern business corporation is. (The same people also made the best documentary ever about journalism and the media, 1992's *Manufacturing Consent*.)

Michael Moore is famous for his documentaries, and while he has received some legitimate criticism — along with boatloads of illegitimate criticism — his work stands up as a vital panorama of economics and political life in America. Blending humor and intelligent analysis, he asks tough questions in movies like *Roger and Me*, *Sicko*, and *Bowling for Columbine* — and he doesn't settle for simplistic answers. His 2009 film *Capitalism: A Love Story* provides an honest look at what capitalism does well, and where it falls apart.

Two other documentaries about economics are also worth your time: Charles Ferguson's 2010 film *Inside Job* is the definitive cinematic work about the 2008 crash on Wall Street. He digs deep to get real answers, and explains them without resorting to childish oversimplification. He followed it with a book two years later called *Predator Nation: Corporate Criminals, Political Corruption, and the Hijacking of America.* The best feature film about the 2008 crash is 2011's *Margin Call,* which features Kevin Spacey and Jeremy Irons as executives at a trading firm dealing with the first days of the disaster. It's confusing and understated, but very well done. On a larger scale, the other must-see documentary about money is a little 2001 movie called **Life and Debt,** about Jamaica's decades-long struggle to keep its economy afloat in the face of incredible pressure from outside forces. It's a dynamic look at how most of the world deals with the economic demands of the US and Europe.

One last documentary deserves mention here: ***The Yes Men Fix the World*** (2009). Two guys set up fake websites where they pretend to represent large corporations (Dow Chemical, Halliburton) and government agencies (Housing and Urban Development). They go on TV and appear at conferences, making outrageous statements that show the horrible reality of the pathetic misdeeds (or negligence) of the organizations they're targeting. On the 20th anniversary of the Bhopal chemical spill in

India, for example, they appeared on BBC News claiming that Dow Chemical was giving billions of dollars to compensate the victims in India. Hilarity, as you can imagine, ensued, along with a drop in Dow's stock price.

Traffic (2000) and *Syriana* (2005) are two superb movies examining complex issues — the drug trade and politics in the Middle East, respectively — with appropriately complex storylines. They also feature excellent performances from Benicio del Toro and Don Cheadle in *Traffic*, and George Clooney and Matt Damon in *Syriana*. They require repeat viewings, and even after several times through I feel a bit lost at certain points. But Stephen Gaghan, who wrote both, weaves together stories from all over the world, showing the intricate heartbreak of these important issues.

Speaking of complex storylines, *The Wire* (2002 - 2008) must certainly be mentioned in any discussion of popular media addressing social issues. Although it's an HBO miniseries and not an actual movie, it stands out as the most cinematic work about drugs in the US. (Plus it put the incomparable Idris Elba on the map.) Avoiding simple good guy / bad guy stereotypes, it starts out following a small group of cops chasing drug dealers in Baltimore. But it quickly becomes a gripping

interrogation of every part of modern life in the city:
schools, government, corruption, courts, business, and
more. President Obama once praised it as his favorite
TV show of all time, and asked for a sixth season.
Creator David Simon said he would do it if Obama
called off the drug war.

Spike Lee is well-known for his movies examining
race (and other issues) in America; his 1989 film *Do the
Right Thing* is a landmark in African-American cinema.
He made two other movies that are also excellent, if less
well-known. I was surprised to see him turn his
attention to the Italian-American community in 1999's
Summer of Sam, about a series of murders in 1977. The
result, however, is a fascinating look at how the threat
of violence affects people in every walk of life. Superb
performances from Mira Sorvino and Adrien Brody also
stand out. One year later Spike returned with
Bamboozled, an over-the-top satire about race in popular
media that was unfairly dismissed by critics and most of
my friends. Using actual blackface performance to
examine the ways in which performers have to "dance
for the bosses" isn't subtle, but it is effective. Plus that
movie let Mos Def show his acting chops, which were
considerable even then.

Fruitvale Station (2013) also failed to get the attention it deserved, although the critics liked it. It tells the true story of Oscar Grant, an unarmed black man who was shot to death by security officers in the Oakland public transit system on New Year's Day 2009. It stars Michael B. Jordan, who played Wallace on *The Wire*, then went on to play Adonis in *Creed* as well as Killmonger in *Black Panther*. *Fruitvale Station* resists sentimentality or simplicity, while still telling a heartfelt — and heartbreaking — story.

Moving in a very different direction, we find **Michael Clayton**, a 2007 movie about the law that intentionally avoids the courtroom. Tilda Swinton won the Oscar for her portrayal of a top executive at a chemical corporation. The movie looks at how corporations relate to the law, and how that relationship affects the rest of us. It digs into the personal elements of people at different levels of this system, and ends with a truly gripping finale. A superb blend of thriller and psychological drama.

I'll end with a series of science fiction movies that deal with politics in unconventional ways. Most people think of **Robocop** (1987) as an over-the-top violent action movie about a cyborg policeman, which it is. But along the way, director Paul Verhoeven also provides the most important science-fiction cinematic look at how we humans interact with technology, especially with regard to money. I can't say more without spoiling things, but if you've stayed away because you think the film lacks serious weight, you're wrong. (The 2014 remake approaches some other interesting issues, but fails to use most of its potential.)

District 9 (2009) also looks like a simple movie, this time about aliens — but it's more. Set in Johannesburg by South-African director Neill Blomkamp, it provides a fascinating analysis of exclusion, oppression, fear, and difference. It's psychologically terrifying and hard to watch; by the third act it loses its direction and becomes a weird buddy action flick. Still, *D9* shows how science fiction can be used to discuss things no other genre can approach. Blomkamp had another great concept with his second movie, 2013's *Elysium,* but it got lost in cliches of the action genre.

Finally I will sing the praises of two movies based on comic books by Alan Moore. Both *V for Vendetta* (2005) and *Watchmen* (2009) start with source material that is complex, confusing, and politically rigorous. Hollywood had to leave things out and change some bits to make them work as films, and some big mistakes were made. The love angle in *V* is hokey, and the change of a final line in *Watchmen* — which I can't name without spoilers — is atrocious. Still, the movies are superb adaptations and provide an excellent look into these worlds. Hugo Weaving — who played Agent Smith in the *Matrix* movies — does a superb job as the charming V, and Natalie Portman brings an electric dynamism (not to mention a gorgeous shaved head) to the role of Evey. The performances in *Watchmen* are also excellent, especially Jackie Earle Haley's gritty turn as Rorschach. The books, as always, are better than the movies — but the movies do a very good job of interrogating issues of government, human nature, and political consequence.

GOOD POLITICAL BOOKS

I could easily list 20 books on each of the topics I've discussed in the chapters above. Instead I'm going to limit myself to two each. Before I do, however, let me quickly promote Aaron McGruder's *Boondocks* comics. If you like the TV show, you must read the comics; start with the collection *A Right To Be Hostile*. I'm also a fan of Diane DiMassa's fiery feminist *Hothead Paisan* comics.

If you want to discover the classic texts of feminism (and you totally should), I'll let you explore Betty Friedan and Simone De Beauvoir and Mary Wollstonecraft on your own. I want to put a word in for two more recent texts: bell hooks' 1981 book ***Ain't I A Woman?*** pays homage to Sojourner Truth and the legacy of black women struggling against sexism and racism. hooks is an engaging writer with straightforward prose. Her book was an important milestone in the literature of enlarging the feminist struggle beyond the domain of well-to-do white women. The other book I will recommend here is a 2001 collection called ***Listen Up: Voices from the Next Feminist Generation***, edited by Barbara Findlen. It gathers essays from many women, telling stories of heartbreak, violence, and overcoming. It addresses sexuality and sexual orientation, gender, class, and dozens of other issues. A superb sampler of the many different ways feminism has moved into the American consciousness. John Stoltenberg's 1989 collection of essays *Refusing To Be A Man* and Ariel Levy's 2005 book *Female Chauvinist Pigs: Women and the Rise of Raunch Culture* are also worth your time. Finally, allow me to shamelessly promote the Wikipedia Featured Article on British suffragette Emmeline Pankhurst, most of which I wrote.

Anarchist theory and practice haven't changed much over the years, so the foundational texts by Mikhail Bakunin and Pierre-Joseph Proudhon are still relevant today. If you read only two books about it, however, I would start with Emma Goldman's 1931 memoir **Living My Life**. It covers her entire life — before her 1936 journey to Spain to resist the fascists there — and contains many important reflections on how anarchism can be lived. (The Wikipedia Featured Article about Goldman is also excellent.) I will also recommend the 2005 book **Chomsky on Anarchism**, which features a series of profound discussions with MIT linguist and anarchist dissident Noam Chomsky, covering everything from state organizations to business structures to education to family dynamics. He speaks with a range and erudition that can be hard to ingest at first, but keep with it and it'll make sense.

Many books have, of course, been written about capitalism, and I recommend that everyone read the writing of Adam Smith — both *The Wealth of Nations* and *Theory of Moral Sentiments* — and Milton Friedman alongside Karl Marx. Forced to pick two, however, I'll recommend more recent books. First is the South Korean-British economist Ha-Joon Chang's superb 2010 book ***23 Things They Don't Tell You About Capitalism***. Using humor, pop culture analogies, rigorous facts and specific examples, he explains why there's no such thing as a free market and how the washing machine changed society more than the internet. The other is a 2012 book from Pulitzer Prize-winning investigative journalists Donald Barlett and James Steele, called ***The Betrayal of the American Dream***. Barlett and Steele broke vital ground in the 1980s with newspaper reporting about the decimated middle class in the US, and unfortunately things have not gotten better in the years since. The authors use plain language to explain how both political parties have aided and abetted the ravaging of American working people and general prosperity. Their earlier books, especially *America: What Went Wrong?*, are also valuable texts. I will also add a shameless plug for two treatises I've written about capitalism — *Global Economics 101: Five Things Everyone Should Know About the IMF, World Bank, and WTO* and the sequel *Global Economics 201: Five More Things Everyone Should Know About International Economics and "Free Trade"*.

There can be no question that classic texts about race in America from WEB DuBois, Frederick Douglass, Black Elk, Manuel Garnio, and others deserve serious attention. As always, however, I'm going to recommend two books from more recent authors. The first is Cornel West's 1994 collection **Race Matters**. Many of the essays address topics specific to their time — the Clarence Thomas hearings, the Crown Heights riots — but West's engaging style and deep sense of history (not to mention the slow progress we've made as a nation) keep them vital today. I will also insist that everyone in the US read Michelle Alexander's 2010 book **The New Jim Crow: Mass Incarceration in the Age of Colorblindness**. She explains how the so-called "drug war" has become the new incarnation of a centuries-old system of oppression and second-class citizenship. Filled with specific examples and mountains of data, she writes clearly and directly, mincing no words and leaving no room for ambiguity. I will also mention the Wikipedia

Featured Article on American hero Harriet Tubman, most of which I wrote.

Although we usually hear about war books, plenty of books have also been written about peace and how to fight against war itself. While foundational texts from Clausewitz and Sun-Tzu are essential for any peacemaker's library, I will recommend two more recent books here. The first is William Blum's 2000 text *Rogue State: A Guide to the World's Only Superpower*. Blum worked in the Department of State before watching the US government violate human rights across the board during the Vietnam War. He devoted himself to research and writing, and has produced various books illuminating the unpleasant truths about US foreign policy. In *Rogue State* he uses the criteria of UN Resolutions — which folks in the US cite frequently when preparing to drop bombs or send troops — to show how frequently our government violates the same world consensus we seek to uphold. I must also recommend the books of Joe Sacco, who has made his life's work comics about war zones around the world, providing street-level reports from Bosnia, Iraq, India, and elsewhere. His 1993 book *Palestine: A Nation Occupied* is a good a place to start. Guy Delisle has also produced some excellent — if less political — comics travelogues from places like North Korea and Jerusalem.

I must confess that I haven't read enough books about LGBTQ issues. One that I can recommend without hesitation, however, is Sarah Schulman's 1998 book **Stagestruck,** in which she explains how Jonathan Larson ripped off and changed her novel *People In Trouble* when he wrote *Rent*. (I interviewed Schulman on my *Didactic SynCast* program in August 2016.) The other is Alison Bechdel's 2006 memoir **Fun Home.** Using remarkable precision and gallons of literary references, Bechdel tells the story of her father's closeted homosexuality and the rage it caused. Bechdel is also the creator of the superb serial comic strip *Dykes to Watch Out For,* which ran from 1983-2008.

Rachel Carson's 1962 book *Silent Spring* gave birth to the modern environmental movement, and (as noted above) Peter Singer's 1975 text *Animal Liberation* is a foundational work in the field of animal rights. (Singer is also featured in a fascinating 2009 documentary film about philosophers called *The Examined Life*.) The two eco-books I will offer here are more recent. The first is **This Changes Everything: Capitalism vs. The Climate** (2014) by Naomi Klein. Boldly challenging us to transform our relationship with nature away from the consumption model so central to capitalism, Klein offers a stark analysis and glimpses of hope. The other is a mix of feminism and animal-rights advocacy from 1990 called *The Sexual Politics of Meat* by Carol Adams. By juxtaposing the ubiquity of sexist and meat-consumptive imagery — often in the same advertisements — Adams presents a powerful way to think about these entwined issues, and a powerful bonus motive to change our diets.

FINAL THOUGHTS: LIVING LIKE AN ACTIVIST

I can't tell you how you should structure your activist life; I can only tell you what works for me. The most important lesson, however, is this: Being an activist should be a deep, integral part of who you are. But it shouldn't be all of you.

Everybody must find their own balance between working to make the world better and enjoying life itself. Neither alone is sufficient. Those who ignore the horrors of the world and "go for self" inevitably make life more difficult for everyone else. Those who devote every waking hour to The Struggle usually burn out, or become bitter, miserable people. I want people to be involved in smart, long-term ways that can be sustained for decades.

The urgency of youth is good for activism. The radical author Abbie Hoffman once said (in a recording I can no longer find, so this is a paraphrase): "We need young people in the front. Young people are impatient.

They want change *now*." We must take care, however, to avoid consuming ourselves entirely in the passionate drive for change. Paradoxical as it may seem, we need to be impatient in the face of the status quo, while also understanding that change takes time. Ani DiFranco put it this way, in her 1993 song "Pick Yer Nose": "I fight with love / and I laugh with rage / You've gotta live light enough to see the humor / and long enough to see some change".

Youthful indignation is a good way for us to check ourselves; too many people abandon their principles as they become adults. Homer Simpson once told his daughter Lisa: "I used to believe in things when I was a kid." Now that I'm supposedly an adult, I wonder what my 15-year-old self would think of me. I think he'd be pretty satisfied with my life so far. Of course, clinging to our youthful mind is not healthy; in 1975 Muhammad Ali said: "The man who views the world at 50 the same as he did at 20 has wasted 30 years of his life." As always, the key is balance.

One popular myth is that young people are impetuous and naive when it comes to politics. As they say: "If you're not liberal when you're 20, you have no heart. If you're not conservative when you're 40, you have no brain." In other words: young people have empathy, which is great — but they have no real stake in the world as it is. Therefore they're willing to support unrealistic causes and impractical ideas. In their 1995 activist anthem "Go", The Indigo Girls said: "Did they tell you it was set in stone? / That you'd end up alone? / Use your years to psych you out? / You're too old to care / You're too young to count".

I call hogwash on this notion. My ideas have evolved during my four decades on the planet, but I didn't abandon my moral principles when I got married and took on a mortgage. In some ways I've become even more radical than I was in my 20s. But I've also gotten smarter about how I express my radicalism. I've come to understand that my indignant rage shouldn't be aimed at individuals — it should be aimed at evil itself: at hypocrisy, injustice, and suffering.

One important step is to find a job or career in the field of attacking the wrongs of the world. It's simply not true that we must decide between making a decent living and doing work that makes the world better. Of course it's much easier to make money if you're aiding or abetting the ills of our civilization, but I can't imagine that anyone reading these words has money as their top priority. I've been lucky to find a stable and secure position as a high school English teacher, incorporating history, knowledge, enlightenment, solidarity, and progress into all of my classes. The intense demands of teaching, unfortunately, don't leave me oodles of free time to invest in other forms of activism, but I do what I can.

And that's the key to living as a life-long activist: Do what you can. Know thyself, as The Oracle told Neo. Recognize when you need a break. Take walks. Meditate. Eat good food. Play games. Treat yo'self from time to time. And then, when your soul is healed and your mind is ready, strap the spiritual armor back on and return to the fight.

Some activists who are more hardcore might call me "soft" or "moderate", but I learned long ago to take such critiques in stride. I will never dismiss them, because they align with the voices in my head insisting that I can — and should — do more. But I've also picked up some voices reminding me of Article 24 in the Universal Declaration of Human Rights: "Everyone has the right to rest and leisure, including reasonable limitation of working hours and periodic holidays with pay." These voices assure me that it's fine for me to limit my working hours and take an occasional holiday.

This work is never done. We'll never achieve a perfect utopia of human harmony, so we must commit to being active throughout our lives, in various forms and flavors. As Richard Thieme wrote in his 2004 piece "My Last Talk with Gary Webb":

> The passion for truth and justice is not a sprint. It's a long-distance run that requires a different kind of training, a different degree of commitment. Our eye must be on a goal that we know we will never reach in our lifetimes.

If you're willing to pursue that goal and join the fight for a better world … well, as Cornel West said at the end of a 1996 speech in St Petersburg, Florida: "I'll be right there with you. Because I'm going down fighting."

GRATITUDE

I'm always nervous to list people at the end of a book, because I'm terrified I will leave someone important out. But I want folks to know how much I appreciate them, so I'm taking the risk. Apologies to anyone I forget.

I must start by thanking my parents and my brother for their insight and guidance while I tried as a child to make sense of the world. From an early age, my folks insisted on kindness and compassion, traits that have served me well all my life. By devoting their lives to education and public safety, they showed me what it means to live your beliefs.

My brother and I grew politically and spiraled around each other for many years, dipping into the same activist circles only occasionally. We both returned to our hometown in Gainesville, Florida for a while before I moved to Wisconsin. That was a great time; we worked shoulder to shoulder on issues related to labor, feminism, and peace, and we were closer than ever before. I'm incredibly fortunate to have a sibling so deeply committed to values of progress and solidarity.

I must also thank my amazing wife Diane. We met through East Timor activism, and our shared intensity to that struggle forged a bond that has never withered. She is smart, funny, and relentlessly devoted to fighting the darkness.

Speaking of East Timor, I want to thank everybody who joined the fight to end that occupation. Kristin Sundell convinced me to attend my first national gathering of any kind, with the East Timor *Action* Network, and I will be forever grateful to her for it. That trip changed my life. I met so many amazing people in ETAN, including Charlie Scheiner, John Miller, Ben Terrall, Yohan and Milena, Joe Nevins, John Roosa, Karen Orenstein, Lynn Frederickson, Nate Osborne, Pam Sexton, Curt Gabrielson, Constâncio and Gabriela Pinto, Erik Gustafson, Jill Sternberg, Tom and Inga Foley, Mike Iltis, Elliot Stokes, and many others.

I'm also grateful to the activists at New College who worked hard to make things happen on our tiny, insulated, sleepy campus — especially Mala Ghoshal, Annie O'Connell, Jess Falcone, Jesse Griest, Sof Ali-Khan, Rosa Ellis, Amy Murphy, Cory Knoettgen, Colleen Butler, Margaret Hughes, and Sheila Bishop. Thanks also to my Gainesville activist friends Joe Courter, Jenny Brown, Aris Polyzos, Howard Rosenfeld, and James Schmidt. Special thanks also to Shae and Garrett Crowell, Josh Heling, Amy Jester, Jon Broad, Doug MacDonald, and Liv Lindenberg.

I want to thank the people I teach beside — too many to name here. The teachers of Sun Prairie High School work hard and look out for each other. I am lucky to be one of them. I also want to thank the members of the Sun Prairie Education Association, our teachers' union. Your solidarity and unity have carried me through some painful moments.

Finally: Much love and thanks to the students who have worked with our school's Amnesty International club. Your willingness to take action for human rights — on top of your heavy school and work schedules — gives me hope. Good luck with the so-called "real world". Please stay in touch.

INDEX